First published in Great Britain 2023 by Farshore
An imprint of HarperCollins*Publishers*,
1 London Bridge Street, London, SE1 9GF
www.farshore.co.uk

HarperCollins*Publishers*
Macken House, 39/40 Mayor Street Upper,
Dublin 1, D01 C9W8, Ireland

BEANO.COM

A Beano Studios Product © DC Thomson Ltd (2023)

Written by Mara Alperin
Design and additional illustration by Matt Carr

Additional imagery used under licence from Shutterstock.com

ISBN 978 0 00 852996 3
Printed and bound in UAE
001

CONTENTS

Note from the Editor 6

Welcome to … Beanotown! 8

Useful Phrases 9

Means of Escape 10

THE SIGHTS OF BEANOTOWN 12

Beanotown-on-Sea 14

Beanoland 16

The Pool! 18

Beanotown Skatepark 20

Beanotown Library 21

Museum 22

Mount Beano 23

Beanotown Cinema 24

Beanotown Zoo 26

Cold Trafford 28

The Park 30

NEIGHBOURHOOD WATCH OUT! 32

The Menaces 33

Dennis 34

Gnasher 35

Dennis Sr 36

Sandra Menace 37

Bea Menace 38

Gran Menace 39

Pesky Pets 40

The Makepeace Family 41

Minnie Makepeace 42

Batmin / Chester the Cat 43

Vicky Makepeace 44

Darren Makepeace 45

The Dawson Family 46

Roger the Dodger 47

Ada Dawson 48

Les Dawson 49

AROUND TOWN 50

Beanotown Bites 52

Rocket Man 53

Har Har's Joke Shop 54

Har Har's Top Tips 56

Prank You and Goodnight! 58

Bogeyman Tours 60

Widl 62

More Shopping 63

Perkins Paperclip Factory 64

Wilburcorp 65

Top Secret Research Station 66

Beanotown Hospital 68

Beanotown's Baby Minder 69

THE LAWS OF BEANOTOWN 70

Beanotown Police Station 72

Angel Face's Casebook 73

Bananaman Fan Mail 74

Elect Mayor Brown 76

Wilbur Brown 77

Walter Brown 78

Muriel Brown / Clawdia 79

EDUCATING BEANOTOWN 80

Mrs Creecher the Headteacher 82

Ralf the Janitor 84

Meet the Olives 86

Meet Class 3C 88

Miss Mistry 90

Familiar Faces 91

Pie Face 92

Rubi 93

Billy Whizz 94

Dangerous Dan 95

Angel Face 96

Bertie 97

JJ 98

Vito 99

The Dinmakers! 100

Class 2B 102

Danny / Mandi 104

Toots / Sidney 105

Scotty / Wilfrid 106

Mahira / Cuthbert 107

Plug / Erbert 108

Freddy / Stevie 109

Sketch Khad / Smiffy 110

Jokes & Pranks 111

BEANOTOWN ODDITIES 112

The Beanotown History Society 114

Beanotown's Secret Tunnels 116

Horrible Hall 118

Town Hall Clock Tower 119

Duck Island 120

Lake Mess 122

Dennis's Den 124

Injury Hill 126

Beanotown Allotments 128

Wildlife Spotter's Guide 129

Squelchy Things 131

The Numskulls 133

THE BIG BEANOTOWN QUIZ 134

Become a Beanotown Resident 140

Goodbye! 142

OH, HELLO THERE! ARE YOU LOST? NO? WELL THEN, I GUESS I'LL PEE THE FIRST TO WELCOME YOU TO BEANOTOWN! (GEDDIT? BECAUSE I'M I.P. DALEY! READ MY NAME OUT LOUD AND IF YOU STILL DON'T GET IT, THEN *GOOD LUCK SURVIVING YOUR FIRST TRIP TO BEANOTOWN!*)

I'VE BEEN INTERVIEWING EVERYONE ABOUT TOWN AND COMPILING STORIES, SO THAT YOU CAN MAKE THE MOST OUT OF YOUR TRIP TO THIS BONKERS PLACE. GOOD LUCK (YOU'LL NEED IT)!

Welcome to... BEANOTOWN!

VISITORS' GUIDE

In a place as cool* as Beanotown, there are naturally many things that outsiders may be baffled by. There are super-secret tunnels, offbeat oddities and pranksters aplenty. You might slip on a fake poo, be chased by an evil carrot and then fall down a trapdoor in the school basement ... and that's just an ordinary Monday!

Beanotown is a great place for anyone who has imagination, loves pranks and wants to hang out in a place where kids rule. This visitors' guide will help you to explore the real Beanotown, stay alert for mischief-makers and bamboozle your enemies – just like a true Beanotown resident.

*cool as in amazing, not cool as in covered in slippery ice. Except for that winter Dennis left the school tap running, and overnight the classrooms turned into an ice-skating rink ...

USEFUL PHRASES

You'll talk like a Beanotown resident in no time with these useful phrases! Regularly using these expressions will help you to:

Speak to locals
Prepare yourself for conversation
Integrate with the residents
Travel through Beanotown with confidence

DON'T FORGET TO **S.P.I.T.!**

Blam – awesome; wonderful. As in: *'Check out my new skateboarding kickflip trick – it's totally blam!'*

Blamazing – incredible; even more blam than just regular blam. As in: *'Check out my new skateboarding kickflip trick, followed by a powerslide – it's totally blamazing!'*

Gnish-gnash gnash! – loosely translates to *'Hi friend, I am hungry and I would like a sausage, so why haven't you fed me one yet?'* Most likely to be used by Gnasher, Dennis's dog.

Knick-knock-no! – that moment when you realise that someone has pranked you by putting itching powder in your knickers, but you can't reach down to scratch your butt because you're carrying a tray of glasses and don't want to knock them over – oh no! (So far in the history of Beanotown, no one has yet uttered this phrase . . . but that does not mean it will not be useful.)

Prankmageddon – the greatest chain of epic pranks ever pulled off in the history of Beanotown pranks (and that's saying a lot)!

Result! – success! As in: 'I hid 12 whoopee cushions in the classroom . . . so when students sat down, they all went off at once. Result!'

Simples! – expression meaning 'This is something that can be done without much difficulty.' It's a lot, er, simpler to just say simples! As in: *'You want me to clap twice? Simples!'*

Super Epic Turbo Cricket – the ultimate super-sport: a bruise-filled combo of football, ice hockey, rugby, cage-fighting and paintball.

FUN FACT: the most recent Super Epic Turbo Cricket Cup was won unexpectedly by Bash Street School.

MEANS OF ESCAPE

It takes less than an hour to get to Beanotown from wherever you live, as long as you travel by skateboard. But that's not the only way to get around . . .

TRAIN

Beanotown Railway Station is open every day, come train or shine. Train drivers screech to a halt and leave faster than Billy Whizz after the school bell rings, so don't dawdle – the conductor doesn't care–iage if you get left behind!

BUS

Look really carefully before sitting down on a Beanotown bus, in case there's a squishy tomato or water balloon on your seat. Hang on tight! The driver, William Bramble (Wilf's dad), is very careful . . . at least, he tries to be careful when he's not busy crashing into the town hall or the mayor's car.

GO-KART

This is the best way to travel for those who don't have time to stop and look at the scenery . . . because there's a 99.7 per cent chance the brakes won't work. But its giant mushy–pea cannon works perfectly every time to break your fall!

8:45 TO MARS

Even Beanotown's finest sometimes need a quick getaway. The 8:45 to Mars zips between Beanotown and the Red Planet for the price of a fake pimple. This ship departs precisely at 8:45, so you'd better planet carefully, so you don't miss it!

HOT AIR BALLOON

If you get stuck, you could always ask Lord Snooty for a ride in his fabulous hot air balloon. This red–and–black striped aircraft will be upgraded with super–speedy WiFi at some point, but when exactly that will be is still up in the air.

HELICOPTER

This belongs to Mayor Wilbur Brown, so don't even think about asking for a ride.

THE SIGHTS OF BEANOTOWN

Ah, the sights of Beantown! Arm yourself with this guide book, a map and 13 loo rolls (you never know when it will come in handy), and spend the day exploring the wonders of this marvellous town!

BEANOTOWN-ON-SEA

Why travel abroad for your summer holidays when you have a beach right on your doorstep? Beanotown-on-Sea is the perfect spot for a picnic on the sand (if you're not bothered by seagulls stealing your lunch) and for dipping your toes in the water (if you don't mind losing one or two of them to a hungry shark).

RELAX-O-METER

MEDIUM

LOW

HIGH

THE LAST TIME I TRIED TO HAVE A RELAXING NAP ON THE BEACH, I WOKE UP BURIED IN THE SAND. WHAT'S MORE, SOMEONE PUT SEAWEED IN ONE SHOE AND THEN WEED IN MY OTHER SHOE. NEVER AGAIN!

MRS CREECHER

For ultimate fun in the sun, just follow these ten simple rules . . .

RULES OF THE BEACH

1. No dogs on beach

Gnasher loves the beach. Just dip him in the water first and tell everyone he's a sea anemone!

2. No shouting

It doesn't say you can't yell, scream or whoop though!

3. No feeding the sharks

Unless it's bits of the Olives' leftover mystery stew. Then it's just recycling, and what grown-up is going to tell you off for recycling?

4. No digging for Greenbeard's lost pirate treasure

Unless you find it, and then it's Greenbeard's found pirate treasure, and it doesn't say you can't dig for that!

5. No knocking over other people's sand sculptures

A better prank is to tunnel a hole beneath them, and let the sculptures cave in on themselves!

6. Beware of submerged objects

Like Billy Whizz after he's done a super-sonic cannonball into the water!

7. No climbing up to the top of the lighthouse to hide from teachers

You're safe – none of the grown-ups have enough puff to make it up all the stairs after you!

8. No replacing people's sunblock with chilli oil, so when they lather up, it really stings

That was ONE time!

9. No peeing in the water

No comment!

10. Rulebreakers will be ~~fined~~ just fine!

BEAN

Beanotown's awesome amusement park

Beanoland is a destination like no other. A place crammed with puketrifying rides, where panicked screams fill the air. Can anyone make it through these rides without losing their lunch?

BEANOTRON 4000 ROLLERCOASTER

The fastest rollercoaster in Beanotown! The track reaches a terrifying height before sending riders hurtling down the 'Drop of Death' at a rate approaching the speed of light.

> NOT BAD FOR AN AMUSEMENT PARK RIDE, BUT A BIT SLOW FOR ME.

> DON'T ASK WHY, BUT I HAD TO PACK A SECOND PAIR OF PANTS.

IT'S A 'MAUL' WORLD AFTER ALL

Whirl and twirl along a rickety old track, while dangerous wild animals chomp at your cart and try to maul you. Will you survive the gravity–

LAND

RALLY RACE CARS

Ready, steady, race! Zoom along the track at high speeds, avoiding potholes, exploding tyres and flaming pots of oil. Some call this one 'dangerous', but only those who survive. (Those who lose consciousness on this ride are strangely quiet about it). Extra points for knocking your mates off the course!

NEXT TIME, I'LL CONVINCE WALTER TO DO THIS AT THE SAME TIME. HA!

THE BOUNCY BUNKERTON CASTLE

You'll feel like royalty as you bounce along to some groovy tunes in this squishy, soft-play castle. Perfect for the little ones!

BOING!

A NICE, SAFE PLACE FOR MY ONE-YEAR-OLD DAUGHTER BEA TO PLAY. WAIT A MINUTE . . . WHERE DID SHE GO? OH HELP – SHE'S UP ON THE BEANOTRON! SOMEONE STOP THAT RIDE. STOP THAT RIDE!

FAMILY DAY PASSES AVAILABLE

Five pukes for the price of four! We hope that your visit is a memorable one!

THE POOL!

Beanotown's swimming pool is legendary for many reasons. Firstly, there's no better place to cool down in the summertime. Also, it boasts several blamazing waterslides, such as The Twister, The Water Beast and The Banana Flume (which is based on a dog's intestines).

And there's one other reason, but you're probably not that interested in reading about it, so maybe skip this section if you know what's good for poo . . . I mean, if you know what's good for you . . .

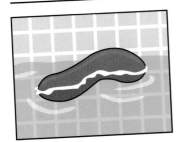

The offending article

Beanotown's legendary swimming pool

EX-POO-SIVE STORY

TODDLER CAUSES MASS POO-NIC WITH CODE-BROWN ALERT

BY WADE MCFLOAT – EVERYONE'S FAVOURITE SWIMMING POOL CORRESPONDENT

I've been making waves reporting on pool perils for forty-three years, but never have I heard a story like this one, so let's dive in!

This fiasco all started in the down-to-earth province of Beanotown (if you haven't been, my sources tell me it's less than an hour away from wherever you live if you travel by skateboard). A certain Dennis Menace Sr took his young daughter on the waterslide . . . but he forgot to put her swim-nappy on. Talk about being lax!

The young toddler, a Miss Bea Menace, then had an accident at the top. What kind of accident, you may ask? Well, the other swimmers rushed out of the pool, calling the resulting mess 'a tor-poo-do'

Let's just say that it was 'the poo-fect storm', and that the whole pool had to be evacuated. It was a stinking tragedy.

It took a full week to clean the pool, so residents had time to spare to share their personal accounts from that smell-ventful day:

Local man: I was relaxing on my pool float like any other day . . . when suddenly everything went brown. I'll never forget it.

Local woman: Last summer, I had my littlest pinky toe bitten off by a great white shark on Beanotown Beach . . . and that was a picnic compared to this!

Dennis Sr: I don't know how that happened . . . um, Bea's never done anything like this before . . . cough, cough . . . Are you sure it was Bea? That grandad over there is looking pretty suspicious if you ask me.

Dennis Jr: Wow, that was even stinkier than the time Dad accidentally opened the washing machine mid-wash and a whole pile of Bea's washable nappies sprayed everyone in the room!

Walter Brown: I happen to have my own swimming pool. I don't need to sputter around at the disgusting public pool with all those commoners.

New species baffles experts

GNAWS SCARES MAYOR'S SON

BY PAUL CLEANER

In unrelated non-poo news, a mysterious 'dogfish' has been spotted doing the doggie paddle in Mayor Wilbur Brown's private swimming pool and is reported to have frightened his son Walter so much that he has decided to stop swimming all together!

BEANOTOWN SKATEPARK

Beanotown skatepark is one of the most popular hangouts in Beanotown. It's very busy after school, at the weekends and during school holidays. It would be popular during school hours too ... except for the fact that it's right next to the school, so teachers make sure nobody tries to sneak on to it during class.

Despite its popularity, the residents of Beanotown appear to be split on whether this park is wheely great or wheely awful ...

A VERY IMPORTANT NOTICE FROM MAYOR WILBUR BROWN:

This skatepark is a local travesty. I've closed it down once, and it would still be closed if it weren't for some obnoxious children. But never fear, here are just some steps of my ingenious, 37-step plan for closing it down – for good this time! Come to the town hall next week to hear the rest and vote in favour of my proposal to bring peace and quiet back to Beanotown!

STEP 1: Replace all skateboards with chalkboards. You can't skate without a skateboard, can you? While we're at it, let's make children use their new chalkboards to do an extra three hours of homework every night.

STEP 2: Change the laws of Beanotown, so that everyone who says the word 'skatepark' has to pay a fee to me.

STEP 3: Redevelop the half-pipe into a half-pine forest, full of songbirds who will be trained to sing tunes loud enough to cover up the unpleasant sounds of Beanotown's unruly children ...

HOLD IT RIGHT THERE. WE AT BEANOTOWN S.O.S. (SAVE OUR SKATEPARK) WON'T LET WILBUR GET AWAY WITH THIS! I'VE GOT A FEW TRICKS UP MY SLEEVE, AND I DON'T JUST MEAN THE BACKSIDE POWERSLIDE. ANYONE WHO SITS DOWN AT THE NEXT TOWN HALL MEETING WILL BE ITCHING TO LEAVE BEFORE THE VOTE TAKES PLACE, IF YOU CATCH MY DRIFT!

BEANOTOWN LIBRARY

Beanotown Library is known as the tallest building in Beanotown. That's because it has the most stories. Ha ha ha. If you don't get it, maybe you should check out the 'Joke Book' section at the library.

(Seriously. Don't blame me if your sense of humour isn't up to scratch!)

COMPLETE BEANO COLLECTION

HISTORY OF BEANOTOWN

HOMEWORK ANSWERS

SPECIAL OFFER! FREE INTERIOR PAGES WITH EVERY BOOK COVER! 100 % YETI APPROVED. TS & CS APPLY.

25,000 BOOKS

4,100 MAGS

32 CHEESE PLANTS

INTERVIEW WITH MRS BINDING, HEAD LIBRARIAN
By Paige Turner

Paige: First, 25,000 books? If we say each book weighs approximately one kilo, then that would be the same weight as . . . twenty grown-up elephants singing, one baby elephant crying, nine grand pianos and a triangle. What a musical marvel that would be!

Mrs Binding: I see you've been reading Useless Facts to Impress Your Friends from our 'Know-it-all' section.

Paige: You must know the collection well. How long have you been working here?

Mrs Binding: Oh, since the library opened. I also work at the Bash Street School Library. The other librarian there is a ghost. She says she's there to haunt it, but I know she loves her job secretly - I can see right through her.

Paige: And you . . . erm, giant shaggy white creature thing, how long have you been working here?

Mrs Binding: This is Biggy Smells, my personal assistant. They dress up as a yeti every day to be our library mascot. Biggy arrived last winter. They check in books faster than anyone I've ever known!

Biggy Smells: Shhhhh!

Paige: Sorry! I guess that's the end of our interview then!

OVERDUE BOOKS

NAME	BOOK TITLE
Dennis	Itching to Try It: Pranks to Befuddle Your Parents
Minnie	War and Peashooters
Pie-Face	Lord of the Pies
Rubi	Great Experimentations
Mahira	Just for Kicks: Football Legends Through History
Eric Wimp	101 Delicious Banana Recipes

MUSEUM

B.U.M. GUIDE
Beanotown's Useful Museum Guide

Only £1

KNIGHT-TIME ROBBERY THWARTED BY BANANAMAN

Tuesday, 11:53 pm

Beanotown Museum nearly lost one of its dustiest treasures when Doctor Gloom tried to make off with a suit of armour rumoured to belong to the knight Sir Render. According to witnesses, Bananaman apprehended the doctor, crying:

MYSTERIOUS VIKING OBJECT IN MUSEUM IDENTIFIED AT LAST!

BY DR RAM PAGE

We all know that the Vikings arrived in Beanotown in 801 A.D. They got straight to work doing important Viking things – they tunnelled out secret ancient tunnels, and carved secret ancient carvings.

But what did Vikings use this strangely curved metal hook for? That has been a mystery for hundreds of years . . . until now.

Using a **Scientific Nasology Optimising Test (S.N.O.T.),** Beanotown's own Professor Von Screwtop has revealed that this object is none other than a Viking nose-picker, likely used by a local tribe. This impressive artefact will be on display for all museum visitors to marvel at.

'This discovery is nothing to sniff at,' said Professor Von Screwtop. 'Nose-picking has been around for thousands of years, and now we can further study how the Vikings' techniques differ from modern methods.'

NEVER TAKE SOMEONE ELSE'S ARMOUR WITHOUT AXING FIRST!

HUE DONE IT?

Wednesday, 9:05 am

Colourful graffiti found painted all over the wall in the left wing of the Beanotown Museum. Police suspect it was finger painted by someone approximately one year old. Anyone with information on this unsightly prank should speak to Sergeant Slipper.

'NOW WE NOSE!' FIND OUT MORE ON THIS STORY ON PAGE 2

MOUNT BEANO

1938 METRES

FART!

Standing at 1,938 metres tall, Mount Beano towers over Beanotown. Just how tall is that, you ask? Well, it's roughly the height of 1,210 snowman balancing on top of each other, or the **maximum height a dog like Gnasher could propel himself to with the world's most powerful fart.**

This snow–tacular mountain is at the heart of all sorts of exciting adventures...

'THERE'S SNOW SNOW ANYWHERE IN THE WORLD LIKE BEANOTOWN SNOW. THE SNOW ON TOP OF MOUNT BEANO IS SUPERIOR SNOW. IT'S PERFECT FOR SNOWBALLS, SLIDES AND SENSATIONAL ADVENTURES!'

PROFESSOR VON SCREWTOP, WORLD-FAMOUS SCIENTIST AND SNOW-IT-ALL

JOIN THE YETI TRACKING EXPEDITION!

Rumours have been racing through Beanotown about the Abominable Beast of Mount Beano – a humongous, hairy creature responsible for throwing giant snowballs, scaring residents and making even the mayor of Beanotown poop his pants.

So think how impressed your friends will be when you spot it! Our expert team have gathered several clues: photographs of giant footprints, samples of the superior snow, and – yes – even giant lumps of Yeti poo. Come and join the hunt!*

GRIZZLY GRILLER'S NATURE SURVIVAL COURSES

What would you do if you were ambushed by three polar bears who stole all your clothes and left you to perish on top of a snowy mountain? Or what about if your enemy is struck by lighting and it gives them the superpower to freeze you with a single glance?

If you don't know the answer to these questions, you are not prepared to survive in nature. But wait – there's still hope! Just sign up for Beanotown TV survival expert Grizzly Griller's Nature Survival Course. We'll throw you into the wild to see if you've got what it takes!*

* Safety not guaranteed.

BEANOTOWN

There is always something to watch in Beanotown, but sometimes you want to escape from real life. Welcome to Beanotown Cinemas, where we invite you to sit back, relax and enjoy the show.

THE ROCK ROCKS!

SERVICE GRUMP-O-METER

LOW | MEDIUM | HIGH

Why is the service so bad?
No one knows.
They like to keep you in the dark.

HOW MUCH FOR THE POPCORN?!

I ♥ STA JAWS

WHAT'S ON?

BRUISE WILLHISS

PIE HARD

AFTER AN EXPLOSION AT THE PIE FACTORY, ONLY ONE POLICEMAN IS BRAVE ENOUGH TO TAKE THE MATTER INTO HIS OWN HANDS. HE BURSTS INSIDE, SHOUTING: 'SLICE TO SEE YOU. DO YOU WANT A PIECE OF ME?' CAN HE RESCUE HIS WIFE AND MAKE IT OUT ALIVE? YIPPIE-PIE-YAY!

FIVE STARS! LOTS OF FIGHT SCENES AND LOTS OF PIES!

CINEMA

VANILLIAM MILKSHAKESPEARE PRESENTS

ROMI-POTATO AND JULI-COURGETTE

Romi-potato is quite the spud, but can he ever be with his starch-crossed lover Juli-courgette? This is a tater-ible movie. Don't bother going, unless you're Pie Face and your pet potato has begged to see it.

EWWW, YUCK, GROSS ROMANCE! ZERO STARS!

RHUBARB DOWNPIPE JR

IRON MANGO

Rony Lark is just an ordinary guy, until one day he accidentally irons a mango to his face. *BLAM! WHAM! ZAP!* Now he's the best fruit-based superhero, Iron Mango! But will he ever defeat the Professional Organisation Of Terrorists (P.O.O.T.)? Yes, he will. Oh wait, we've just spoiled the movie for you.

HOW DARE YOU! I'M THE BEST FRUIT-BASED SUPERHERO! ZERO STARS!

BEANOTOWN ZOO

'I was just watching the chimps fling their poo, and then POOF – it happened!' claimed a local boy in a stripy top.

'Oooo ooo aah aahh!' claimed a second witness, who refused to say anything further to this well-regarded reporter.

According to witnesses, the toddler somehow became trapped in the chimp enclosure, where she mooned the public and was promptly flung from chimp to chimp. After several minutes of monkeying around, she was thrown out and landed on an elephant. Tusk, tusk – has no one taught them any manners?

Soon after, the child slipped into the snake house. Would this young baby soon be hisssstory? No – she wasn't even rattled. She passed through the crocodile enclosure withou getting snappish. But whe she finally soared into the lio enclosure, it was time to pre

BABY SET LOOSE IN ZOO!

BY ANNIE MEL

. . . .

MAMMALS! MADNESS! MAYHEM! ON SATURDAY, A LITTLE MENACE HAD A BRUSH WITH DISASTER WHEN SHE FELL INTO THE CHIMP ENCLOSURE . . . AND THINGS WENT APE-SOLUTELY CRAZY!

paws on this perilous adventure. The toddler was spotted snuggled up with the cubs. They were all just lion around.

'I'm so glad she's okay,' the stripy-topped boy concluded. 'But let the record show that I was never scared, not even for a moment.'

It should be noted that witnesses claim the stripy-topped boy fainted at least twice, and had to have his face licked to be brought round.

'Don't worry, the zoo is perfectly safe,' said Mayor Wilbur Brown. 'Everyone should keep buying tickets, so I can make more money due to my controlling share in Beanotown Zoo . . . I mean, everyone should keep coming because it's a fun and educational experience.'

One thing is for sure – it was truly a wild day!

WHO THREW THE POO?

BY JIM PENZEE

Scientists have discovered that throwing poo is a sign of intelligence in chimpanzees, and is used to communicate. This is true of chimpanzees worldwide, and the Beanotown primates are no different.

There have been several other notable poo-throwers in the history of Beanotown. Dennis Menace achieved a record distance when he **lobbed a fake poo 12.2 metres.** Kate 'Toots' Pye **catapulted her fake poo an amazing 27.6 metres.**

Meanwhile, Rubi Von Screwtop has been busy inventing the 'poomerang' that once thrown, comes back. The first prototype failed, but she claims the next version is a solid number two.

COLD TRAFFORD

Home of BEANOTOWN UNTIED F.C.

To some, it's 'Cold Trafford' and to others it's 'The Theatre of Screams', but whatever you call it, you'll have a ball at Beanotown's Football Stadium. Here is the home of Beanotown Untied (it was supposed to be Beanotown United, but their speeling wuzn't verry god), where the fans are super-loyal and the players are . . . well, they're still alive, mostly. You've got to celebrate what counts.

COLD TRAFFORD IS ALSO HOME TO AN ANNUAL SPORTS DAY, BUT TO BE HONEST WE HAVE NO IDEA WHAT SPORTS THEY ACTUALLY ARE!

B.U.F.C.

KICKUS ET RUNNIUM

0 - 12

SMASHEM TOWN FOOTBALL CLUB

Date: Last Saturday
Attendance: Not sure, it was a bit foggy.

Scorers: Lost count.
Red Cards: Didn't dare send anyone off!

A Kick in the Grass: An Interview by Hattie Trick

Following Beanotown Untied's 12–0 loss to Smashem Town, I caught up with Beanotown's own defender Penn Elty-Kix to chat about the club's hopes and dreams. Because that's all you have when you lose time after time after time . . .

Penn Elty-Kix: Wait a minute, you said this was going to be an upbeat interview!

Hattie Trick: Oops, sorry about that. Once I get the ball rolling talking about your losing record, it's tough to get back on track.

Penn Elty-Kix: It's not all bad news! All our players have been thinking about the game a lot recently, and that's led to everyone dribbling more.

Hattie Trick: You mean like dribbling the ball?

Penn Elty-Kix: No, I mean dribbling from our mouths. Because we're concentrating so hard, you see.

Hattie Trick: Right.

Penn Elty-Kix: And our keeper just got a brand-new pair of boots. I'm sure that will make a huge difference.

Hattie Trick: Please tell me these are football boots . . .

Penn Elty-Kix: Wellington boots, actually. He's been dribbling so much, the area around the goal is starting to flood. Luckily, the wellies keep his feet nice and dry!

Hattie Trick: Help me out here! Can you give the fans any hope?

Penn Elty-Kix: I don't want to jinx it, but there's an up-and-coming youth star named Mahira Salim. She was signed up after a scout saw her playing keepie-uppie with a teddy bear at Nursery. In fact, her brother Mani is on the team – but we try not to talk about his record for own-goals. She might be Beanotown Untied's only shot at avoiding relegation.

Hattie Trick: I'll cross my fingers – we all hope you can kick that habit of losing!

THE PARK

Beanotown Park is a beautiful spot for a picnic by the flowers, a walk around the duck pond or a friendly chat on a park bench. Just don't spend too long there or you're likely to get tangled up in someone's prank, as Beanotown Park is a hotspot for the local pranksters. Don't say we didn't warn you!

Beanotown's Pretty Awesome Race in the Park? P.A.R.P.

The first person to complete all ten challenges wins a dinner for two at **Beanotown Burgers,** plus 26 minutes of bragging rights.

1. Start at the fountain. Dive to the bottom to retrieve one of Bea's swimming nappies that fell off here. (Don't forget to wear your scuba gear – or, better yet, a hazmat suit!).

2. Race over to the swings. When you get there, swing until you're at the very top, then flick your shoe into someone's picnic.

3. Dig a hole in the sandpit and bury a jammy biscuit. You'll need to come back for this later, so try to remember where you left it.

4. Find the hedge that Parky Bowles the parkkeeper has carved to look like a giant squirrel, and put an orange cone on its head.

5. Choose the least suspicious-looking park bench and leave a fully-inflated whoopee cushion behind. You can't move on to step 6 until someone has sat down with a PFFFFFT!

6. Crawl across the grass to the stream. Catch an old leather boot (with a fishing pole or with your teeth – your choice!).

7. Climb the tree marked 'No Climbing'. Blow raspberries at people walking past until you get caught.

8. Using a water pistol, spray Mayor Brown's trousers, so it looks like he's had an accident. If he sees you, whistle and pretend to be a bird.

9. Win a game of duck–duck–goose against one of the animals at the duck pond. (We should warn you – they've been training every night for the past six years, and they don't give up easily!)

10. Go back to the sandpit and dig up your jammy biscuit. If necessary, fend off Gnasher, Gnipper or any other dogs who may also have uncovered it. Grab this and run across the finish line. First across wins!

Anyone caught cheating, dodging or skiving will be sent back to the start and must hop on one foot for the remainder of the day.

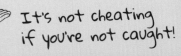

It's not cheating if you're not caught!

B.U.F.F.O.O.N. PROJECT

MEMO

**From the desk of the esteemed *
Mayor Wilbur Brown**

Recently, I took it upon myself to initiate the **B.U.F.F.O.O.N. project: Beanotown's United Forum For Obliterating Obnoxious Neighbours.**

This is a brilliant scheme that I have dreamed up to identify Beanotown's most troublesome neighbours – and then banish them to the edge of town. This will make more space for the right sort of lot (i.e. me and my family), and make Beanotown a more tolerable place to live.

Unfortunately, the whole campaign budget was spent on designing the B.U.F.F.O.O.N. logo. At this time, there is no funding left to remove such obnoxious neighbours.

*in the words of Mayor Wilbur Brown himself.

FOR YOUR EYES ONLY

In the meantime, stay alert for menaces. And stay off my lawn, all of you!

THE MENACES

One of the oldest and best-known families in Beanotown, the Menace clan is filled with troublemakers. Menaces by name, Menaces by nature – at least, that's what the neighbours say!

NEIGHBOURHOOD WATCH · B.U.F.F.O.O.N. PROJECT

DENNIS

Dennis is Beanotown's Prankmaster-General. He takes this role very seriously, leaving no rubber cockroach behind and no whoopee cushion un-parped. He also seems to believe this sort of thing makes life more fun and exciting, so expect to see him laughing as he lies in wait. He thinks he's so clever!

Dennis is a seasoned skateboarder, and you'll probably spot him whizzing around the streets of Beanotown. If you come into contact with the town's Number 1 Menace, you're in for a wild ride!

Natural habitat

51 Gasworks Road

How to recognise him

Spikey black hair, red-and-black jumper, has that look of a ten-year-old who's about to set off a stink bomb.

When you can avoid him

9am-3:30pm Monday-Friday: Dennis should be in school . . . unless he's used the secret tunnels to escape class.

Where you can avoid him

Avoid the treehouse in the garden at all costs, unless you want to be the victim of Dennis's stinky socks or catapult attack (or, worse: his launch-a-stinky-sock-from-the-catapult attack).

What to do if you come into contact

Take cover behind a large pile of homework, so he can't aim his pea-shooter at you. (Dennis rarely misses, but he's likely to run away from the sight of homework!).

WHAT PEOPLE SAY

'The terror of Beanotown!'
Walter Brown, neighbour

'I can't prove it, but I'm sure Dennis is the culprit of the latest stink bomb that went off in the teacher's lounge!' Mrs Creecher, Headteacher

'Dennis has a great imagination – he can pull pranks and have fun anytime. Not everyone has that skill!' Gran, Dennis's grandmother

MISCHIEF-O-METER

8

GNASHER

Dennis's loyal pet has a coat that is tougher than barbed wire and teeth that can gnash through a concrete block. This is not someone you want to drop your homework in front of - he's known to rip through reports in seconds!

Gnasher has been with Dennis since he was a puppy (since Gnasher was a puppy, that is . . . Dennis was never a puppy). Gnasher can understand Dennis, and Dennis thinks he can understand Gnasher, so what could ever go wrong?

Natural habitat

51 Gasworks Road

How to recognise him

Look out for the small, shaggy hound with hair like barbed wire.

Known disguises

Dennis's backpack

Where you can avoid him

When Gnasher's not at Dennis's side, he might be snoozing in his kennel or sniffing the sausages outside Butch Butcher's shop. To be safe, you should always guard your sausages in these places - or any place!

What to do if you come into contact

Shout 'Bathtime!' and start spraying perfume everywhere. If you accidentally left your Canine-Clean-2000 spray at home, try holding up a lead. Gnasher hates dog leads almost as much as he hates baths!

WHAT PEOPLE SAY

'He's chasing me again. ARGH!' Postman Josh

'His coat is the perfect place for a nice nap.'
The Golden Menace Flea (itchus terribilis)

'Gnasher is the best friend a boy could have.'
Dennis, best friend

DENNIS SR

Dennis Sr was never a menace like his son Dennis. He's sure he's a responsible grown-up. If you're asking about that time he painted jelly on the walls of Bash Street School back when he was ten, you're probably confusing him with someone else.

Dennis Sr was voted laziest employee at Perkins' Paperclip factory for regularly falling asleep on the job. Neighbours are warned not to ask for his help with DIY - apparently, you're better off risking electrocution.

Natural habitat

51 Gasworks Road

How to recognise him

Wild black hair, grumpy expression, often grumbling at Dennis.

When you can avoid him

9am-5pm Monday-Friday: Dennis Sr should be safely tucked away at work, though be warned that he often leaves the house late.

Where you can avoid him

Dennis Sr can often be found in his death trap of a shed. Do not go here.

What to do if you come into contact

Start flapping your arms and making swan noises, and he'll probably retreat. Dennis Sr is terrified of swans.

WHAT PEOPLE SAY

'When is he going to mow that lawn?'
Vicky Makepeace, neighbour and sister-in-law

'I have no idea what Sandra sees in him.'
Wilbur Brown, neighbour

'I guess he's the most fun dad I have.'
Dennis, son

MISCHIEF-O-METER

8.5

7 SANDRA MENACE

Dennis and Bea's mother Sandra is calm and well-organised, and she helps keep the rest of the Menaces in line. But don't let that fool you into thinking she's harmless. Sandra has a secret career of 'borrowing' priceless pieces of artwork. She does this to help out the rich, so they don't have so much clutter in their houses.

Sandra is also the Chief of Staff for the mayor of Beanotown, and gives Wilbur Brown lots of good advice. He hardly ever listens, though!

Natural habitat

51 Gasworks Road

How to recognise her

Bright orange hair, a calm smile while keeping a firm eye on Dennis and Bea.

Avoid her if

You have valuable paintings (even if you're sure they're hidden in an unbreakable safe guarded by two drooling Alsatians).

What to do if you come into contact

Ask her about her children and nod politely. Do not mention the priceless jewelled statue that's been passed down through your family for generations.

WHAT PEOPLE SAY

'Of course I've already done my homework, Mum! Erm, why do you ask?' Dennis, son

'I'm sure there's nothing suspicious hidden in my little sister's secret cupboard. It's probably just an extra mop or spare loo roll . . .' Vicky Makepeace, sister and best friend

'I can neither confirm nor deny that Sandra is a fully qualified ninja.' Darius 'Dark' Cobra, CIA

Natural habitat

51 Gasworks Road

How to recognise her

Messy black hair, yellow hairband, pink dummy, whiffy nappies.

When you can avoid her

11am-12pm daily: Bea should be napping, however, don't be fooled by her sweet baby face and the dummy in her mouth – she's still capable of producing strong smells while sleeping.

Where you can avoid her

Go somewhere up high. Bea won't be able to reach you . . . yet.

What to do if you come into contact

Hold your nose. Hold your breath. Run. If you run away, she might not be able to crawl quickly enough to catch up.

BEA MENACE

Dennis's little sister may be small, but Bea's ability to fill a nappy on demand is nothing to sniff at. In fact, you're better off not sniffing at all when you're within three metres of her.

Bea has been described by neighbours as 'a mini menace' and 'nearly as destructive as Dennis'. You might be able to distract her with a bedtime story, but don't even think about giving it a happy ending.

WHAT PEOPLE SAY

'Her fingerpainting is dreadful, truly dreadful.' Walter Brown, neighbour

'Will she ever stop bashing me with her rattle?' Dennis Sr, dad

'Bea just filled *another* one?' Sandra, mum

9

GRAN MENACE

6.5

Dennis's gran is also Dennis Sr's mum. She remembers all the antics Dennis Sr used to get up to as a boy (maybe it's in their blood?). Gran always stands up for Dennis and Bea, and doesn't think anyone should take life too seriously.

Gran owns a Harley Davidson motorbike and has been crowned 'Most Dangerous Gran Award' ten years running, so you've got to keep an eye on her!

Natural habitat

67 Sutherland Crescent

How to recognise her

Candy-pink hair, square-rim glasses, often riding her motorbike.

Avoid her if

You've got somewhere to be and don't have the time for a long tea break with lots of stories about the good old days, when Dennis Sr was just a little boy sprinkling sneezing powder on the tulips in Beanotown Park.

Also take care if you have a sugar intolerance - her cups of tea are very sweet!

What to do if you come into contact

Keep a sound mind while she offers you obscure wisdom such as 'fancy gold and silver butters no parsnips' or 'a biscuit a day keeps the doctor away*'.

· · · · · · · **WHAT PEOPLE SAY** · · · · · · ·

'Er, is that her natural hair colour?'
Darren Makepeace, relative

'Can I have another biscuit, Gran?'
Dennis, grandson

'Grandmothers should stay at home and knit all day, not go riding off on their motorcycles. What a disgrace!' Walter Brown, concerned resident of Beanotown

*Actually, this one is probably true. And even if it's not scientifically proven, can you really take that risk?

You're probably thinking: wait, there's more Menaces to keep track of? Watch out for these!

GNIPPER

PESKY PETS

Gnasher has six children: Gnipper, Gnancy, Gnatasha, Gnaomi, Gnanette and Gnorah. Only Gnipper lives in Beanotown though (phew!). The others live in Gnottingham.

(Don't even ask about Gnasher's gnieces and gnephews . . .)

Gnipper has the same rough coat and powerful teeth as Gnasher. Gnipper can often be found at the side of Bea. They're probably up to something - and it's likely to involve lots and lots of drool.

DASHER

Dasher is Dennis's giant spider. You'll recognise him because . . . well, he's a giant spider with a big red stripe. It's not like you're going to get him confused with a goldfish! Try not to let Dasher bug you. Because he's a spider, and technically spiders aren't bugs.

MISCHIEF-O-METER
6.5

RASHER

MISCHIEF-O-METER
5.5

Rasher is a pig who spends half the year living with Dennis and the other half with Gran. Don't let her near your garden if you don't want it to be rolled over and dug up everywhere. Rasher's special talent is making a mess and scoffing turnips. She likes most vegetables, but favours the ones that turnip the most often.

THE MAKEPEACE FAMILY

The Makepeaces are another well-known family in Beanotown. Luckily for you, five of the Makepeace children (Michael, Martin, Mark, Morris and Max) have all left home. Unfortunately, Minnie - Dennis's cousin - has enough mischief in her to rival even the Menace family . . .

MINNIE MAKEPEACE

Minnie has a special knack for unleashing devastating and destructive pranks. You might see her setting them up alongside her friends Dennis and Roger, but don't be fooled – the prank was probably Minnie's plan. And even if it wasn't, Minnie will claim it was. She's the quickest thinking problem-creator in all of Beanotown, if she does say so herself.

Natural habitat

54 Gasworks Road

How to recognise her

Two red bows in her ginger hair, black-and-red jumper (which looks nothing like Dennis's red-and-black jumper), black hat with red bobble.

Where you can avoid her

Minnie is not one to sit around, so it will take some serious planning – and a good pinch of luck – to keep away from her. She might be setting up her latest prank or she might be tiptoeing through the tunnels below Beanotown. The best way to work out her location is to listen out for the yells!

What to do if you come into contact

First, try to ignore those big eyes and innocent expression. Minnie is up to something! Your best bet is to make a quick escape, or to recommend frilly, pink dresses. Minnie doesn't like frilly, pink things.

WHOOPEE CUSHION

WHAT PEOPLE SAY

'Minnie is loyal, tough and – quite frankly – brilliant!' Minnie Makepeace

'Minnie is the glue that holds the Beanotown gang together!' Minnie Makepeace

'Without a doubt, Minnie is the best shot in Beanotown. Probably in the world.' Minnie Makepeace

BATMIN

When Minnie dons her mask and cape, she becomes Batmin - a shadowy superhero who prowls the dark streets of Beanotown, delivering justice with an expertly pulled-off prank. Well . . . superhero might have been pushing it a bit. She is super-good at pranks though, so watch out the next time you consider being a litterbug - Batmin might be waiting in the bushes to put a litter of bugs in your pants!

CHESTER THE CAT

Chester would love nothing more than a life of purrfect peace and catnaps. Alas, he is Minnie's cat. Instead, he often gets dragged from his slumber to partake in her latest prank - or sometimes be the victim of it! If you see Chester out on the street, be aware and do NOT stroke him. He will not be outside willingly - he is most likely the decoy in Minnie's latest prank. RUN!

PHUT!

EXAMPLE OF PEA-SHOOTING ACTION

MINNIE'S ROOM

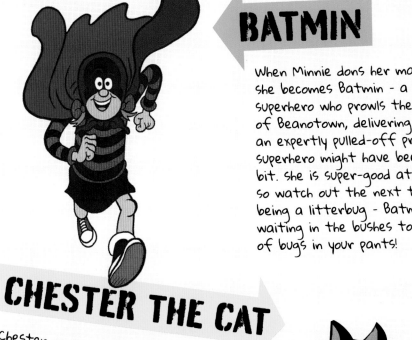

MINXING WEEK ON WEEK 2016

STOPPED UNTIL JUNE 2021!

POCKET MONEY

DAD'S STRESS-RELATED HAIR LOSS

HAIRY   BALDY

MINXING HIT LIST

INNOCENT LOOK

PRACTISE!

BEANO

MINXING BILLS

PEAS

SOPPY GIRLY RUBBISH

ALIBIS FOR THE MODERN MINX

WHO ME?!! INNOCENT EXPLANATIONS FOR THE BUSY MINX

MINXING SUPPLIES (MONDAY)

ESCAPE HATCH!

SPARE HATS

VICKY MAKEPEACE

Minnie's mum is enthusiastic about everything. A mum of six, she loves to keep busy. And who wouldn't want to try her new line-up of hobbies: gymnastics, followed by orienteering, followed by flower arranging, followed by insect collecting, followed by pottery making ... and all before breakfast?

How to recognise her

Oversized purple jumper, often trying to organise large groups of people.

Avoid her if

You just want to lounge in front of the TV for an hour (or day or two) and not sign up for your 15th new club this week.

What to do if you come into contact

It's too late. You're going to be dragged along to the next rock-spotter meeting, so you might as well stop fighting it and try to enjoy it.

WHAT PEOPLE SAY

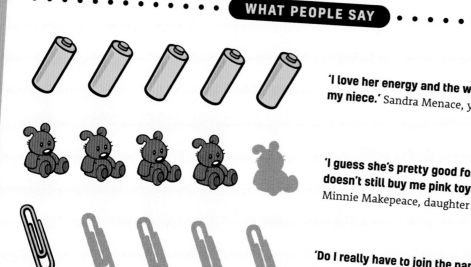

'I love her energy and the way she supports my niece.' Sandra Menace, younger sister

'I guess she's pretty good for a mum. She doesn't still buy me pink toys like Dad.' Minnie Makepeace, daughter

'Do I really have to join the paperclip pals club?' Dennis Sr, employee and brother-in-law

DARREN MAKEPEACE

How to recognise him

Orange hair, goofy 'dad' smile.

Avoid him if

You don't want to hear any financial advice or grumblings about why certain children don't have better manners.

What to do if you come into contact

Darren doesn't like surprises, so do something unexpected: roll around and act like a wiggling worm, pretend that you've gone blind or scream every time he blinks.

Darren Makepeace loves being a dad. He's been subscribing to 'Dad Monthly' for the past ten years! When he's not fixing things that Minnie has broken, he likes making models from matchsticks, staring at spreadsheets and practising judo (he's a black belt - hi-YAH!).

When Minnie was born, he bought a lot of cuddly, pink teddies . . . and he's still looking for someone to play with them. (And by play, he doesn't mean cut their heads off to launch in a catapult!).

MISCHIEF-O-METER

4

WHAT PEOPLE SAY

'He's a great Dad, but when will he realise that farting when we pull his finger doesn't count as a magic trick?' Mark Makepeace, son

'I wish he would spend less time telling fairy stories and more time helping me with my pranks.' Minnie Makepeace, daughter

'A good father doesn't need to read 'Dad Monthly'. A good father knows he's a good father because that's what he goes around telling everyone.' Wilbur Brown, neighbour

THE DAWSON FAMILY

The Dawsons live further down on Gasworks Road. Ada and Les have always followed the rules, and dislike trying anything new. That's probably why their son Roger is so very inventive!

B.U.F.F.O.O.N. PROJECT

ROGER'S ROOM

SUPER VAC! SUCKS UP EVERYTHING WHEN MUM WANTS YOUR ROOM TIDIED UP... INCLUDING DODGE CAT!

DISGUISES FOR DASTARDLY DODGES

STILTS FOR TALL DODGES

'WIDE AWAKE' GLASSES

BLACK PAPER TO STICK ON DAD'S WINDOW. IT WILL MAKE HIM SLEEP IN... HE'LL THINK IT'S STILL NIGHT TIME!

WANTED $100 REWARD

DODGES VOL. 1 MILLION

GET TEACHERS BANGED UP!

YE VERY OLDE DODGE SCROLL

ROGER THE DODGER

Roger the Dodger always has a trick up his sleeve. He uses all his wits (and unfortunately for you, he has quite a lot) to perform dodges - getting his own way, or getting out of doing things. He takes great care planning and setting up the perfect prank that lets him avoid doing any hard work!

Even when he's not organising his own dodges, he's still dangerous. Roger runs a well-hidden Wiki site that logs every dodge ever created, so that others may learn from his wisdom.

Natural habitat

14 Gasworks Road

How to recognise him

Red-and-black chequered jumper, lazy smile.

How you can avoid him

In the mornings - Roger will do anything to get out of getting up early (beware of the 'black paper on the window to pretend it's nighttime' trick or the 'wide-awake glasses' hack), so you're fairly safe before 11am. Or even noon.

What to do if you come into contact

Don't - under any circumstance - ask him to do something, because he's guaranteed to dodge it with a prank at your expense. You're better off distracting him with a jammy biscuit and making a quiet escape.

MISCHIEF-O-METER

8

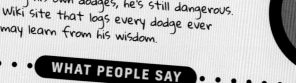

WHAT PEOPLE SAY

'Not too bad at skiving (not as good as me, of course), but he puts way too much effort into setting up his pranks.' Minnie, friend and fellow prankster

'I do wish he'd try getting up just a bit earlier in the mornings!' Les Dawson, father

'I'm so proud to have another dodger in the family to carry on the dodges. I've passed down my dodge library of 850 books, by the way.' Roger's grandad

Natural habitat

14 Gasworks Road

How to recognise her

Blonde hair, often driving a sports car.

Avoid her if

You're not in a rush. Because Ada's favourite thing to say is 'Hurry up, hurry up, hurry up!'

What to do if you come into contact

Get as far away from the road as you can and cover your ears. Ada is known for zooming around in her sports car and she loves hearing the sound of its tyres screeching on the road.

ADA DAWSON

Ada Dawson likes to get things done . . . and she likes them done NOW! You'll spot her telling Roger's dad and Roger what needs doing and when, as she finds them both to be a bit disorganised and lazy!

WHAT PEOPLE SAY

'I love how organised she is, and how much she respects the rules. It's one of the reasons I fell in love with her.'
Les Dawson, husband

'I like her a latte – she's bean my best customer ever since we opened!'
Mo Kalatte, barista at Beanotown Beans Coffee Club

'Goodness, her sports car is rather loud, isn't it? It's not a bad ride, but it's no motorbike.' Gran Menace, neighbour

LES DAWSON

Some people think they always know the best way to do things. Les Dawson is one of those people. He's not afraid to remind Roger of this, because he's quite sure that you can't dodge everything. On the other hand, if Roger's dodges help him get out of having to clean the loo . . . well, who would complain about that?

Natural habitat

14 Gasworks Road

How to recognise him

Grey hair, bushy moustache.

Avoid him if

You're quite happy with the way your shelves are organised, thank you very much, and don't need someone to tell you how to make it better.

What to do if you come into contact

Les can't stand chaos, so if you throw a deck of cards into the air, he'll patiently play 52-card pick-up while putting them all back in order. You can sneak away while this is happening.

MISCHIEF-O-METER

4

WHAT PEOPLE SAY

'He still doesn't know that it was me that set all the clocks back that one time, so we got to lie in until 2pm.'
Roger the Doger, son

'He really is quite good at making sure every one of Perkins Factory paperclips is made the right way.' Vicky Makepeace, colleague

'His moustache looks a bit silly.'
Dennis Menace Sr, neighbour

After a day exploring the more riveting sites such as the Museum and Beanotown Park, you'll want to take some time to eat, shop and limp* like a local.

*This is bound to happen after Dennis slips a pinecone into your left shoe. But don't pine over it for too long – just put your best foot forwards and get back out there on your walking tour!

There's so much to do, and this guide is packed with ideas and inspiration – everything you need to experience the true Beanotown!

Beanotown Bites

If you ask someone in Beanotown for a dinner recommendation, they'll give you great advice: Eat. If you need more guidance than that, look no further than our guide to Beanotown's best bites!

BEANOTOWN BURGERS

NEW

NEW
BUY ONE
GET ONE!
(ER...THAT'S IT!)

HAPPY MEAL

SAD MEAL

THIS WEEK'S SPECIAL
BATTERED COD!
OUCH!

NEW

DRIVE THRU LANE
(JUST OPENED)

FRESH FRUIT

CASH ONLY (OR COPIES OF THE BEANO)

TIP JAR

CHICKEN IN A BUCKET

KITCHEN HYGIENE RULE BOOK

HELP!

SUPER FAST FOOD DISPENSER

NOT HP SAUCE

THE CALAMITY JAMES MEMORIAL MOP

GHERKIN DISPOSAL UNIT (STOP ADDING THEM - WE HATE THEM!)

LUNCHTIME BAN

WANTED DO YOU KNOW THIS DOG?

ASK ABOUT OUR THICK CHIPS! Duh.

WE ONLY USE MATURE CHEDDAR! EAT YOUR GREENS.

CAUTION WET FLOOR (NOTE TO SMIFFY... THIS IS NOT A INSTRUCTION)

FROM THE ALL YOU CAN EAT BUFFET!

ERBERT'S ORDERING STOOL

KANGAROO BURGER

Beanotown Burgers may not look like much on the outside – it may not look like much on the inside, either – but the burgers taste awesome! When you're feeling hungry, come along for the most fun inside a bun. Your money back if not completely satis–fried.

'This is the best place to eat in town! If you want the best chicken burger, look no feather than here.'
D. Menace

'Sausages? I did gnot steal any of their sausages! I would gnever do that . . . oh wait, is that a new salami?'

DJ PERI-PERI'S VEGGIE WRAPS

Yo! Wrap it up, wrap it in, let me begin. Our wraps make you grin, spilt sauce on yo' chin!

STARBUTT'S COFFEE ★ STARBUTT'S COFFEE ★ STARBUTT'S COFFEE

We serve all your favourite hot drinks that go in one end and out the other. Order yours before 9am for the bottomless special!

Taste the best of Beanotown's pastries with local guide, **Pie Face!** He provides a foodie surprise, you pay for all his pies!

BEANOTOWN 🎺 BUGLE

ROCKET MAN OWNER VOWS TO REOPEN AFTER ZOMBIE VEG ATTACK

BY REGGIE TARIAN

MINNIE TAKES ON A BROCCOLI-ZOMBIE

It was a sad morning when owner **Veg Dwight** arrived at his store in the centre of Beanotown to find the windows smashed and the shop ransacked. Information leeked to the press indicates the culprits were human-sized zombie vegetables created in a gardening experiment gone wrong.

'I was devastated to see the destruction,' Dwight said. 'Even the artichokes left behind had their hearts broken.'

This isn't the first time Dwight's shop has bean in a sticky situation. Earlier this year, Bananaman threw a tantrum (and some tomatoes) after an argument with Appleman about whether a tomato is a fruit or a vegetable. The damage took Dwight several cans of tomato paste to repair.

Despite the debris, Dwight said he wanted to romaine calm. **'First I was up all night tossing and turning more than a garden-fresh corn salad. Then I thought – why not be like the corn and play it by ear? I put a big sign out front to ask others to peas help me rebuild it.'**

LOCAL HERO BILLY WHIZZ RACED TO THE RESCUE

Fortunately for Dwight, help arrived in the form of the speeding red blur Billy Whizz. Although ten-year-old Whizz claims that he'd prefer to eat 'fast food', his pet tortoise Tillie loves a good leaf of kale. Whizz whizzed back and forth through Beanotown collecting the materials Dwight needed to rebuild his shop, and got back before Dwight could say **'I'm in a pickle.'** Later that day, Rocket Man was back open for business!

Dwight concluded, **'Lettuce rejoice! Thanks to Billy, I vow to continue growing my produce ethically and enthusiastically.'**

If you're hungry for more, head down to Rocket Man today!

Har Har's

THE BEST JOKE SHOP IN BEANOTOWN IS HAR HAR'S, WHICH IS OWNED BY THE CHANDRA FAMILY. 'A FAMILY THAT PRANKS TOGETHER STAYS TOGETHER' IS THEIR FAMILY MOTTO. WITH SO MANY MASTERS IN THE ART OF PRANKING AROUND TOWN, HAR HAR'S IS NEVER SHORT OF BUSINESS.

WATER BALLOONS

Say 'H2–OH YEAH!' with ten different colours of reinforced–rubber balloons that can be filled with not just water, but jam, slime or tomato sauce. Make a splash this summer!

HAR HAR'S ULTIMATE SLIME

What time is it? Slime time! The squishiest, squelchiest reusable goo – perfect for slipping into handbags or biscuit tins.

ITCHING POWDER

ITCHING POWDER

Sprinkle, scratch, repeat. Need we say anymore?

RED-HOT CHILLI GOBSTOPPERS

Mayhem in your mouth! Terror for your tastebuds! Your tongue will never be the same again.

FAKE POO

Choose from human, dog, cow or – for extreme pranksters only – elephant. Please note: no real poos were harmed in the manufacturing of this prank.

LIME-GREEN FAKE SNOT

It's snot as sticky as you think – and it comes in three citrus burst flavours!

WIDE-AWAKE GLASSES

There's no need to stay awake in class when these glasses can pull it off for you! (For snorers, check out our range of socks that make soothing songbird sounds to cover up your snores.)

'The best glasses I've ever seen!' Roger the Dodger

GAG IN A BAG

It's a surprise!

Joke Shop

PRACTICAL PRANKS FOR PASSIONATE PRANKSTERS

FAKE FLIES
Drop one in your enemies' ice cream to hear them scream, or place on top of their pie to see them cry. (And then pinch the food for yourself when they run away!)

WHOOPEE CUSHION
Time to whoop! Time to pee! (Ok, so these won't actually make you wee.) If you're here, you already know what our premium whoopee cushions do – it's a work of fart.

SNAKE IN A JAR
Twist this innocent-looking jar of preserved sprouts and out jumps a fake python. Guaranteed to make hiss–tory as one of your top pranks.

IN STOCK, FOR NOW!

OPEN

JOKES · PRANKS · GAGS

Someone's gonna get a sur-PIES!

Har Har's Top Tips

Pranks a Bunch!

WE AT HAR HAR'S JOKE SHOP CAN SELL YOU ALL THE PRANKS YOU CAN CARRY IN YOUR 'PRANKS A BUNCH!' REUSABLE TOTE BAG, BUT IT TAKES MORE THAN A FOAM-IN-YOUR-MOUTH SWEETIE OR TWO TO BECOME A TRUE PRANKMASTER GENERAL. IN THE NAME OF PLAYFUL PRANKING EVERYWHERE, HERE ARE SOME OF OUR HAR HAR TOP TIPS AND TRICKS!

1 Never use the same prank twice on the same person in one day. Otherwise, they'll be expecting it. The best pranks are the ones that no one can see coming!

Hari Chandra aka Mr Har Har!

I RUN HAR HAR'S JOKE SHOP WITH SOME HELP FROM MY CHILDREN, HARSHA, HEENA AND HANI. I SAY HELP, BUT THEY SEEM TO BE MORE INTERESTED IN PLAYING WITH THE PRODUCTS AND PLANNING PRANKS THAN SELLING ANY!

POP!

2 A prank should never injure someone. We mean it. The nurses and doctors at St Somewhere Hospital are busy enough looking after Calamity James.

3 Never take credit for someone else's prank. There is a code of honour amongst pranksters. Besides, you don't want to end up in detention for someone else's failed scheme!

4 Never underestimate the power of a fake poo. Some people will scream. Others will faint. Some will just hold their nose. Either way, it's a pranking classic.

And finally...

5 A family that pranks together stays together. This is Har Har's motto, because pranks are way more fun when done in cahoots with your family and friends!

Hani

Harsha

PRANK YOU AND GOODNIGHT!
Spotlight on the Chandra Family

by Joe King

In this issue of Pranking Weekly, we meet the Chandra Family from Beanotown: Hari and Sahana Chandra, and their children Harsha, Heena and Hani. The Chandras run Har Har's Joke Shop, and they are all laughing it up!

'My family test every prank before it goes on the shop floor,' said Mr Chandra. 'It's a real team effort! Our theme of the month is "The Joke is on Shoe", and we're featuring creepy–crawly sole–suckers that stick to your trainers, and magnetic laces that tie themselves together. Have a nice trip home from the shop!'

Find out more about the family, including their favourite pranks (which may serve as inspiration for our readers)!

Hari Chandra

Likes:
Wearing brightly coloured suits, playing practical jokes on his family

Dislikes:
Too many rules and anything that's boring

Favourite prank:
Replacing the loo roll with a jelly loo roll

Sahana Chandra

Likes:
Doing arts and crafts with recycled materials, teaching yoga

Dislikes:
Breaking up squabbles between her children

Favourite prank:
Hiding a whoopee cushion under a yoga mat

Heena Chandra

Age: 13

Likes:
Hanging out with her friends, designing her own clothes

Dislikes:
Doing homework, bad-hair days

Favourite prank:
Replacing her dad's alarm clock with the super-squirter alarm

Hani Chandra

Age: 9

Likes:
Football, dinosaurs, computer games

Dislikes:
His sisters when they get stressy with him

Favourite prank:
Putting fake pimples on his older sisters while they're asleep – often the cause of them being stressy with him

Harsha Chandra

Age: 10

Likes:
Filming videos for You-Hoo of her best pranks in action

Dislikes:
Schoolwork, wearing dresses

Favourite prank:
Leaving a creepy fake finger in someone's cup of tea

Har's Char

Bogeyman Tours

- Looking for a **hauntingly** good time?
- Ready to put the **'oo'** in spooky?
- Want to boogie with a **bogeyman**?

Come along to Bunkerton Castle for the most terror–ific tour around!

Earl Marmaduke Bunkerton, known to his friends as 'Lord Snooty', is a proper 9–year–old lord who lives in Bunkerton Castle with his Aunt Matilda and Parkinson the butler.

He also lives in the most haunted house in Beanotown (and it's not just Parkinson in disguise … HONEST!)

I SCREAM, YOU SCREAM,

Tour Schedule

9am–1pm
Light Fright
Are you easily uneasy? Involving only mild jumps and funny bumps, this tour is perfect for the Walter Browns of this world.

1pm–6pm
Fairly Scary
Feeling overconfident? Unwisely brave? Come along for this afternoon tour, full of tolerable terrors. It might be dinnertime for the bogeyman, but we're fairly sure that it only eats human bogies . . . where it gets them is still a mystery!

6pm–9am
Extreme Screams
Are you a queen of screams? A knight of frights? Then put your courage to the test and spend the entire night in Bunkerton Castle. Last until the morning without screaming, and you'll get your money back!

WE SCREAM, BOGIES!

Widl is Beanotown's biggest supermarket. You can buy anything there – at a price that's nice – from affordable garden furniture to giant inflatable sausages to flat-pack time machines*.

Widl

Widl is
OPEN 24 HOURS
seven days a week, so turn up any time for some of these eye-popping, jaw-dropping bargains!

10% OFF
DRAMATIC CAPES

Swish and swoop like an evil villain plotting world domination, all while looking fabulous and feeling smug about having saved a whopping 10%!

BOGOF!

BLACK-AND-RED JUMPERS

100% exclusive to Widl. Never seen anywhere else! We are totally, utterly, completely sure that you will stand out in this one-of-a-kind item of clothing.

ELECTRIC SCOOTERS

Buy one today, and we'll throw in a spare battery for free! That's an extra 16.5 minutes of scooting on us!

EMPLOYEE PICK OF THE WEEK

50% OFF
HEART-SHAPED MIRRORS

Perfect for the whole family to use together! Sorry, no refunds offered if the mirror wears out because you admire yourself over a hundred times a day.

OPEN ALL HOURS

REUSABLE BAGS

Buy ten reusable bags and we'll give you a free re-reusable bag to carry your reusable bags home in!

POSHLY POSH'S CHOCOLATE BISCUITS

Buy one get one half-eaten. This offer really takes the biscuit!

FARTNITE
FARTNITE LEGENDS OF THE WHIFF

Be the first to buy the latest game here!

*In case you want to travel back to prehistoric times and sit comfortably in your new sun lounger while fighting off a Pterodactyl with an inflatable sausage, duh.

BUTCH'S BUTCHERS

THE WONDER OF STEW!

Meat Butch (also known as Wes Pretend). He is Beanotown's leading butcher and Elvis–impersonator, and he loves meat tender. We can't help falling in love with his range of top–class topsides and I suppose his sausages. You'll find yourself rockin' and chicken casserollin' all night long . . . ok, you get it, right? He likes Elvis Presley.

I'VE GNEVER MET A SAUSAGE HERE I DIDN'T LIKE.

YOU AIN'T NOTHING BUT A HOT DOG!

'HIS PIES ARE NICE. THEY'RE VERY *FILLING*.'

Pie Face

COME IN, TAKE A SEAT! *

CHAIRISHED CHAIRS

Nobody looks after your BUM like we do!

WHETHER YOU'RE LOOKING FOR SOMETHING TOO HARD, TOO SOFT OR JUST RIGHT, WE'VE GOT EXACTLY THE THING TO *CHAIR* YOU UP.

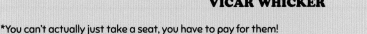

'I found the perfect set of church pews that are so uncomfortable, even Roger the Dodger can't fall asleep on them. I highly recommend this shop for all vicars!'

VICAR WHICKER

*You can't actually just take a seat, you have to pay for them!

Sometimes Beanotown's adults are working hard, and sometimes they are hardly working!*

*Either way, they're grown up and have lost their sense of humour – two things that Dennis Menace will never accept himself!

PERKINS PAPER LIP FACTORY

The Paperclip Factory is a pillar of the community, producing tens of thousands of paperclips a year. The workers here are all very attached to their work!

NOTABLE EMPLOYEES

DENNIS MENACE SENIOR
Quality Control Supervisor

VICKY MAKEPEACE
HR Manager

STAFF ENTRANCE

I NEVER REALLY LOVED PAPERCLIPS, BUT IT PAYS THE BILLS.

KEEP ON CLIPPING!

I ♥ PAPER CLIPS!

keep it together with perkins paperclips!

ABANDON HOPE ALL WHO ENTER HERE!

TOP SECRET RESEARCH STATION

You didn't hear about Beanotown's Top Secret Research Station from us. Sure, it has a cool-looking space rocket and launch pad, and even an extra-terrestrial communication centre, but it's all secret! It's tucked away in Area 50.5 and guarded by a zombie-resistant barrier and a large sign that says:

TOP SECRET KEEP OUT!

TELESCOPE

VIEWING PLATFORM

WEATHER STATION

SOLAR PANELS

But if you're in the mood for geeking out, just ring the doorbell and Professor Wolfgang Norbert Von Screwtop – Beanotown's top scientist – will invite you in for a cup of tea and a chat about his latest experiments. They're all going just fine, you see. Don't worry about the slime oozing out of that test tube – we're **98.4%** sure it's completely harmless.

Professor Von Screwtop doesn't like to brag, but he has four degrees (Quantum Physics, Advanced Chemistry, IT and Awesome Space Farts), three PhDs (Maths, Physics and Super-Hard Chemistry) and a bronze Beanotown-on-Sea Swimming Gala medal.

When he's not working in his laboratory late at night, doing cool scientist stuff (such as inventing a jet-fuelled skateboard that's powered by the phrase 'Dennis, please slow down!'), he enjoys a simple chat about rocket science with his daughter, Rubidium.

Professor Von Screwtop's
INVENTION YARD SALE

Hello and good afternoon, residents of Beanotown! Professor Von Screwtop here. I love mucking about in my Top Secret Research Station, coming up with brilliant inventions. But it's getting a bit crowded in here with the new equipment I've just acquired from Lab Geeks Mail-Order Scientific Equipment Catalogue. It would be a huge help if you could pop round to my Top Secret Research Station (just look for the 'KEEP OUT' signs) this weekend for my Old Inventions Yard Sale. You just never know what you might find.

TOP SALE ITEMS INCLUDE:

ANTI-SHARK CUSTARD POWDER
No fins, no fuss. Just add one teaspoon per ocean, for a sweet, lumpy custard that repels sharks.

BOGEY HOTEL
For lone bogeys and family groupings alike, this natural home with a water-powered generator will provide a great place for your bogeys to hibernate during spring-cleaning season.

BOGEY SLIME
Tired of your bogeys drying out? This slime not only looks and feels like a giant fresh bogey, but tastes like it too!

EXTENDABLE, GLOW-IN-THE-DARK REFRIGERATOR
Never stumble about your house in the dark in search of a midnight snack (or two) again!

GRAVI-TEAPOT
Why tip the pot to pour tea out when it could flow upside-down instead? Perfect for serving a nice cup of Lady Grey to the bats on your ceiling.

ROBOTIC TRAMPOLINE
It bounces even when you can't. Or won't. In fact, it seems to bounce the fastest when you just want to stand still, so watch your step.

AND TO SWEETEN THE DEAL, I'LL THROW IN A FREE CARRIES-ITSELF-HOME BAG WITH EACH OLD INVENTION YOU BUY. YES, I AM INDEED A GENIUS!

BEANOTOWN HOSPITAL (St. Somewhere)

St. Somewhere, Beanotown's hospital, is the busiest hospital in the country. It's a world-leader in treatment of injuries caused by slipping on banana peels or pianos falling on people's heads. This is mostly because **Calamity James** lives nearby, and this sort of thing happens to him A LOT. The staff keep a bed ready for him at all times . . .

PATIENT PROFILE:

Name: Calamity James

Age: 9

Address: 13 Lucky Lane

Next-of-kin: Felicity James (mother)

Hospital visit record – page 427

10th June – Patient was struck by lightning during a freak storm. Our records indicate this is the 14th time this has happened. Advised to stay inside during future freak storms and avoid holding metal poles.

13th June – Patient was stung by a fire ant when he reached down to pick up a four-leaf clover. Advised to be more careful around venomous insects.

19th June – Patient dropped an anvil on his foot. After he finally managed to free his foot, he forgot to look where he was going and bashed into a stack of tyres. Advised to refrain from picking up any more anvils, even if they look 'really interesting and totally safe'.

26th June – Patient slipped in a puddle of super-spicy sauce at Beanotown Burgers. When he tried to steady himself, he tripped on the mop and slid across the floor like a bowling ball, knocking over ten tables in the process. Advised to be more careful around 'Caution: Wet Floor' signs.

1st July – Patient was the victim of a mysterious incident involving the escape of Ellis the Elephant from Beanotown Zoo. After being chased through the town centre and successfuly avoiding being trampled, he got a paper cut from his ticket to the zoo. Advised to carry more plasters with him (as clearly two dozen is not enough).

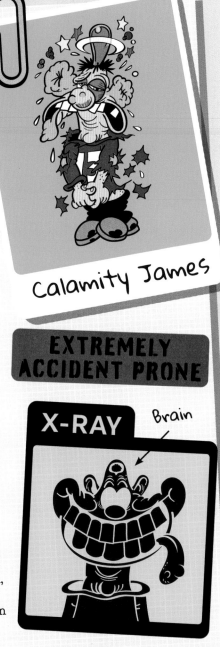

Calamity James

EXTREMELY ACCIDENT PRONE

X-RAY — Brain

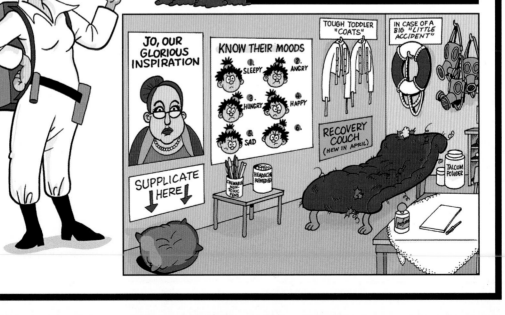

THE LAWS OF BEANOTOWN

There are some unusual laws in Beanotown, which visitors might find disconcerting at first. For instance, all toasters launch toast way up in the air, just like they should (and if they don't, you can bet they'll be arrested and fined – they're toast).

Luckily for visitors, the laws are as clear as the thick chocolate spread that often accompanies toast. Pay close attention to the pages in this section, and you'll be just fine.

BEANOTOWN POLICE STATION

In case of an emergency, you may think you want to call for help. If you do, you may find yourself dialling 999, only to watch the police run away, while calling for Beanotown's local fruit-based superhero, Bananaman. You may then see Bananaman bungling things up (but never fear, he'll live to fly another day).

BANANAMAN

You may have, for instance, needed your cat saving from a tree, and while your cat is now out of said tree, it was because it decided that the risk of falling was preferable to being squished by your car, that is now parked in the tree instead.

Are you sure you need to report a crime? Really? All right, if that's what you want to do, then read on . . .

Beanotown's Police Station is in the centre of town. It has been voted

'MOST UNHELPFUL PLACE TO GO FOR HELP'

the past four years running.

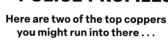

POLICE PROFILES

Here are two of the top coppers you might run into there . . .

NAME:
Police Chief
O'Reilly

AGE: Old enough
to know better

PROUDEST MOMENT:
Managing to not
be turned into a
supervillain by the
evil General Blight

**BIGGEST
INCONVENIENCE:**
Dennis Menace

SUPER-SKILL:
Using the
Bananaphone
to call Bananaman
for help whenever
there's trouble
in Beanotown

BIGGEST CASE:
Stopping the
Forces of Badness
from overwhelming
Beanotown

NAME:
Sergeant Stanley
Slipper

AGE: 58

**PROUDEST
MOMENT:** Getting
his third stripe

**BIGGEST
INCONVENIENCE:**
The bunions on
his feet

SUPER-SKILL:
Droning on about
rules and regulations
for hours, while
writing everything
down in his police
notebook

BIGGEST CASE:
Discovering who
stole the statue
from the plinth in
the town square
(still unsolved)

ANGEL FACE'S CASEBOOK

If you report a crime – for instance, if you see a masked figure chopping down trees in Beanotown Park and laughing evilly – and the police are stumped by it, you can always try Angel Face's Investigating Agency. Her office is above her father Daniel De Testa's garage, and her rates are very reasonable: a small amount of her detecting time will only cost you a biscuit or two.

Monday lunchtime, 12:02pm

MISSING BROWNIE

Sidney Pye reported a missing brownie. Told him I'd do some sleuthing and by the end of the day, tell him who ate his treat for the price of a brownie. I've had two brownies today – another good day on the beat! (Note: My sidekick Jenny keeps reminding me to stop leaving crumbs behind as evidence.)

LOST GUITAR

Thursday morning, 9:35am

Pie Face came to see me again. (Last week, I solved 'The Mystery of the Soggy Bottom' and he's back already.) This time, he's misplaced his bass guitar, even though the Dinmakers are playing in the skatepark tonight. I told him the crime was bassless, but Pie Face promised to write a new song about me, 'Guardian Angel Face', so something's gotta be done. I'll call it 'The Case of the Missing Bass'.

BIG STINK

Friday night, 8:13pm

Residents of Beanotown reported strange lights and smells coming from Fartmoor. There were even rumours of growling sounds and what looked like a giant dog's paw print. My theory is this incident has something to do with toxic waste being created at WilburCorp's dirty power plant. I really should sneak down to Fartmoor and check it out . . . but what's in it for me?

BANANAMAN®

FAN MAIL!

Everyone's talking about Bananaman, Beanotown's top fruit-based superhero. Whenever Beanotown is in danger, Bananaman is just a phone call on the Bananaphone away. He has phenomenally huge strength – and a phenomenally small brain.

Although crime never sleeps and Bananaman's list of supervillain enemies is as long as Scotty's oversized tie, Bananaman still takes time to correspond with his (mostly) adoring fans.

Dear Bananaman
Wow! You are so cool!
I wish I could be big and strong just like you. My mummy already bought me a dramatic cape from Widl (on sale!)
What else do I have to do to become a superhero?
from little timmy
(age 5 ½)

c/o Eric Wimp
29 Acacia Road,
Beanotown

Dear Little Timmy,
Being a superhero is as easy as splitting a banana. Anyone can do it! All you have to do is run around with your pants on top of your trousers, and you'll save the world in no time!

From,
Your favourite handsome, clever, humble hero,
Bananaman

Dear Bananaman,
You've saved the day again!
Thank you for your services
to Beanotown.
From,
Police Chief O'Reilly

P.S. Just a thought, what about
you call me sometime? We could
go out for a banana smoothie
and talk about all the baddies
I've helped you defeat by
calling you up.

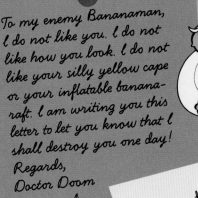

To my enemy Bananaman,
I do not like you. I do not
like how you look. I do not
like your silly yellow cape
or your inflatable banana-
raft. I am writing you this
letter to let you know that I
shall destroy you one day!
Regards,
Doctor Doom

Dear Doctor Doom,
I do not find you
a-peeling either.
From,
Bananaman

Dear Bananaman,
Has anyone else noticed that you and Eric Wimp are
never in the same place at the same time?
I find it all a bit strange, and will be looking into
whether this is some sort of conspiracy.
Yours,
Angel Face, of Angel Face's Investigating Agency

c/o Eric Wimp
29 Acacia Road,
Beanotown

Dear Police Chief O'Reilly,
Thank you for your kind letter.
I'm a very busy top banana, what with
saving Beanotown and testing out my new
gadgets with their ba-nanotechnology.
Maybe one day!

From,
The Hero of Beanotown, Bananaman

Dear Angel Face,
I have no idea what you mean. There
is no conspiracy. I have never even
heard of Eric the Wimp, he's just told
me that he has never heard of me
either. The fact that Eric disappears
at the exact moment I arrive is
nothing more than a coincidence. Your
latest theory is simply bananas.
From,
Bananaman

THE MAYOR'S OFFICE · BEANOTOWN ·

ELECT MAYOR BROWN or ELSE ZILLIONS of ZOMBIES will LOOM over EVERYONE

Wilbur Brown is the mayor of Beanotown, and you'll find his office in the town hall. You'll have to use the stairs to get up to it, though, because the lift is reserved for the mayor himself. Wilbur is a very busy man – what with spending his day puffing out his chest and making other people feel small – but he'll very generously make time for you if you're super important and/or super rich.

LISTEN UP, BEANOTOWN! ELECTIONS ARE COMING UP AND ONLY MAYOR BROWN HAS WHAT IT TAKES TO PROTECT YOU FROM THE ZILLIONS OF EVIL ZOMBIES WHO WILL LOOM OVER YOU AND YOUR FAMILIES, DESTROYING YOUR LIVES AND MAKING CREEPY, HOWLING NOISES WHILE YOU TRY TO WATCH TV.

VOTE FOR MAYOR BROWN – OR ELSE!

Dear Mayor Brown,
I'm sure your new **CAMPAIGN POSTERS** will really strike fear into the hearts of citizens in Beanotown, forcing them to vote for you. In the meantime, I'll keep working on developing that secret serum to turn zillions of people into looming zombies, just in case.
    Yours,
    Dr Pfooflepfeffer

Don't believe everything that Mayor Brown has to say about himself! We at **S.T.I.N.K.B.O.M.B.** (**Super Team of Intelligent, Nifty Kids, warning others to Beware Of Mayor Brown**) are gathering intel on what people really think about Mayor Brown . . .

S.T.I.N.K. B.O.M.B.

★ ★ MEET THE CANDIDATE FOR MAYOR ★ ★

Name:

WILBUR BROWN

Current Job:

MAYOR OF BEANOTOWN

Motto:

'ME FIRST'

Where to find him:

IN THE MAYOR'S OFFICE, OF COURSE

How to recognise him:

THAT BIG, STRONG MAN SITTING BEHIND THE MAYOR'S DESK, WEARING AN EXPENSIVE SUIT AND TIE

Why do I want to be mayor? Well in my current job – as the Best Mayor Ever of Beanotown – I work tirelessly to make Beanotown into the kind of place that important people want to call their home. While I'm on that topic, there are a few unimportant people still here in Beanotown, and it would be nice if they could all go somewhere else. And they should take the noisy, smelly skate park with them!

S.T.I.N.K.B.O.M.B. FILES

Wilbur Brown is the snootiest groan-up in Beanotown. He thinks that he is above everyone else, and that the rules don't apply to him. Wilbur Brown will do anything just to get his own way.

MEET THE CANDIDATE'S FAMILY

★ ★   ★ ★

Name:

WALTER BROWN

Relation:

WILBUR BROWN'S ONLY CHILD

Motto:

'JUST WAIT UNTIL MY FATHER HEARS ABOUT THIS!'

Where to find him:

WHEN HE'S NOT STUDYING FOR A SCHOOL TEST, YOU'LL FIND WALTER RELAXING BESIDE HIS FAMILY'S SWIMMING POOL OR PLOTTING REVENGE ON DENNIS WITH HIS FAITHFUL SIDEKICK, BERTIE

How to recognise him:

THAT TALL KID FROM CLASS 3C WITH GLASSES AND A SUPER-SMUG SMILE

Why should my father be mayor? He's the most important person in Beanotown, which makes me the second most important person in Beanotown. It's true – I really am superior to all my classmates in every way. And Daddy is really rich, so he can buy me lots of things.

S.T.I.N.K.B.O.M.B. FILES

Walter never stops boasting about his rich and powerful family. He's a spoiled bully and the worst squealer. The only person worse for Wilbur's job as mayor would be Walter himself!

MEET THE CANDIDATE'S FAMILY

⭐⭐ ⭐⭐

Name:

MURIEL BROWN

Relation:

WILBUR BROWN'S WIFE

Motto:

'WILBUR FIRST!'

Where to find her:

WATCHING HER FAVOURITE SOAP OPERAS (WHENEVER WALTER AND WILBUR ARE OUT)

How to recognise her:

SHE ALWAYS WEARS A SMART BROWN BLAZER AND CARRIES A BRIGHT-PINK HANDBAG

> Why should my husband be mayor? Well, he works very hard and gets things done that brings in lots of money. Plus it's his dream, and I'll support him all the way. Go, Wilbur!

Name:

CLAWDIA

Relation:

THE BROWN FAMILY'S CAT

Motto:

'HISSS!'

Where to find her:

GLARING AT YOU FROM DOWN BY HER OWNERS' ANKLES

How to recognise her:

BY THE CLAW MARKS SHE LEAVES ON YOUR ARM, SHOULD YOU BE FOOLISH ENOUGH TO PET HER

S.T.I.N.K.B.O.M.B. FILES

Mrs Brown is so busy supporting her husband and son that she doesn't have time to notice how evil they are!

Though easily the prettiest member of the family, do not be fooled by Clawdia's looks: beneath her silky fur is purr evil! She is not scared to get her claws out to get what she wants, just like the rest of her family.

EDUCATING BEANOTOWN

In Beanotown, all the coolest kids go to Bash Street School (and there are 250 of them). The other ones go to Beanotown Academy, which always finishes at the top of the school league tables, but they have strict rules, ugly uniforms and a 'no questions allowed' policy. Plus they have a school song to sing every morning. So the cool kids at Bash Street School are happy* where they are.

*Happy is a relatively inaccurate word to describe how the Bash Street School pupils feel. A better word would be 'not really that happy to be in school in the first place, but begrudgingly accepting that things could be much worse'... except that's not a word; it's 21 words.

Bash Street School is full of weird whiffs, nasty noises and chewing-gum-lined corridors. The school has been rebuilt 24 times (so far) due to incidents including angry ducks, custard explosions and a runaway digger.

HEAD BUSTERS FILE

Name:
Mrs Creecher

Job:
Head Teacher

Age:
No idea (never ask)

Bash Street School is run by Headteacher Mrs Creecher. Some call her 'formidable' and others just say she is 'someone quite forceful, who has the power to make you dread school even more' (which is, in fact, the definition of formidable . . . so it looks like everyone is in agreement).

When a new Headteacher starts at a school, rumours about them will fly faster than Bananaman on the way to rescue a lost banana tree. Here at Head Busters, we investigate to give you the scoop on what is the truth about Mrs Edna Creecher, and what is just a rumour.

YER AFF YER HEID!

TOP SECRET!

82

BASH STREET SCHOOL

Myth	Explanation	
		⚪ Truth
		⚫ Rumour
Mrs Creecher is from Scotland.	She was a wee lass in the Highlands once, and you'll often hear her say things to her students like 'Yer aff yer heid!'* *Translation: You're off your head!** **Wait a minute, is she talking to us at Head Busters? We can't be off our head! Then we'd just be Busters without Heads! ***Double Translation: You're out of your mind! ****Ohh . . . Just like Mrs Creecher, then!	
Mrs Creecher lives at Bash Street School and sleeps underneath her desk every night.	She might live at the school or she might live somewhere in Beanotown – we at Head Busters have not been able to confirm this, and we may never know.	
Mrs Creecher knows every single school rule off by heart.	There are 923 rules in the school rule book, and we've heard her recite them in alphabetic order, then backwards, then in order of how often a student tries to get away with breaking one.	
Mrs Creecher once punched a duck-billed platypus and stole its bill.	We have yet to see any evidence of this. In fact, we don't even know where this rumour came from. Maybe we started it just for fun?	
Mrs Creecher has below-average eyesight.	We've tested this by stealing her glasses. The problem is, we tripped on the way out and she managed to get her glasses back, identify us, and put us in detention for the rest of the week. Sadly, that means no more time to investigate any further rumours about Mrs Creecher!	

BASH STREET SCHOOL

HEAD BUSTERS FILE

Name:

Ralf Chustace

Job:

Janitor

Age:

Not telling

Phew, we managed to survive detention with Mrs Creecher! And those bathroom floors that we had to scrub with our own toothbrushes are finally clean. Speaking of bathroom floors, our next exclusive is with Ralf the Janitor. What ridiculous rumours have you heard about him? It's time to get busting!

I'M CLEANING UP AROUND HERE!

Winston is a singularly paw-culiar cat and has been Bash Street School's cat for as long as anyone can remember. How old is he, you might be wondering? No one knows. Here's what we do know, however.

He earns his keep by assisting Ralf the Janitor around the school, which mostly involves twiddling with radiator valves and hitting the boiler with spanners, though he is very good at mopping the floors.

He has his own office in the basement, that is rumoured to be bigger than Mrs Creecher's and Ralf's combined. His favourite meal is Olive Sprat's curried pilchard's, followed by Olive Pratt's sardine custard. No one else can tell the difference between these two dishes.

WINSTON THE CAT

BASH STREET SCHOOL

Myth	Explanation	
		⚪ Truth ⚫ Rumour
Ralf is the school janitor.	I mean, the mop and overalls are a dead giveaway. You should have been able to figure that one out for yourself!	
Ralf himself used to be a student at Bash Street School.	This is probably true. He has been around at Bash Street School for as long as anyone can remember. And it's not unheard of – many of the staff here were once students themselves (such as Miss Mistry of Class 3C).	
Ralf has a part-time gig as a super-secret agent working for the King.	We can't say for sure whether this is true or not. All we can say is don't believe everything you read online, but we have noticed that the way he waves with his elbows is rather distinctive . . .	
Ralf's best friend is the school cat Winston, who performs music late at night in the music room when no one else is listening.	We tried to record this using our high-tech microphones, but somehow we got the wires tangled and they fell into Ralf's mop bucket and the whole system short-circuited. Still, Winston's rendition of 'Tiny Dancer' on the trombone brought a tear to the eye.	
It was Ralf – not one of the students – who wrapped Mr Teacher's desk in tin foil that time.	Ralf would not confirm or deny this, but our sources do indicate that he loves a good prank!	

FOR YOUR EYES ONLY!

MEET THE OLIVES

There are two dinner ladies at Bash Street School, and though they're both called Olive, they couldn't be more different – Olive Sprat's food is awfully inedible and Olive Pratt's food is inedibly awful. Their daily menu causes gas, groans and gurgling tummies.

OLIVE SPRAT

Dear Olive Pratt,

Happy Dinner Lady Appreciation Day! I'm sure you'll get hundreds of cards from the students for being the best dinner lady ever – they're probably just lost in the post. But you are certainly my favourite dinner lady, and you'd butter believe it!

Before you came to Bash Street School, I had bean struggling to cook for so many students, and I couldn't keep up with all the kids screaming and running away to tell their friends how yummy the food was. And then you got the job here, and I was so berry excited. You're like a soup-er hero in an apron covered with ketchup stains, singing beautifully into your reinforced wooden spoon. No one can overcook a salad like you can!

Your biggest flan,
Olive Sprat

Dear Olive Sprat,

Happy Dinner Lady Appreciation Day to you, too! I'm sure you'll get piles of cards from the students, once they've finished digesting your delicious slop-of-the-day.

We make a beautiful pear, you and me. You taught me everything I know about the school, and I'm forever grape-ful. When the students arrive this afternoon to sing 'Ode to Olive Sprat the Dinner lady', I'll be the loudest voice of them all!

Your favourite colleague-flower,
Olive Pratt

OLIVE PRATT

FLOUR

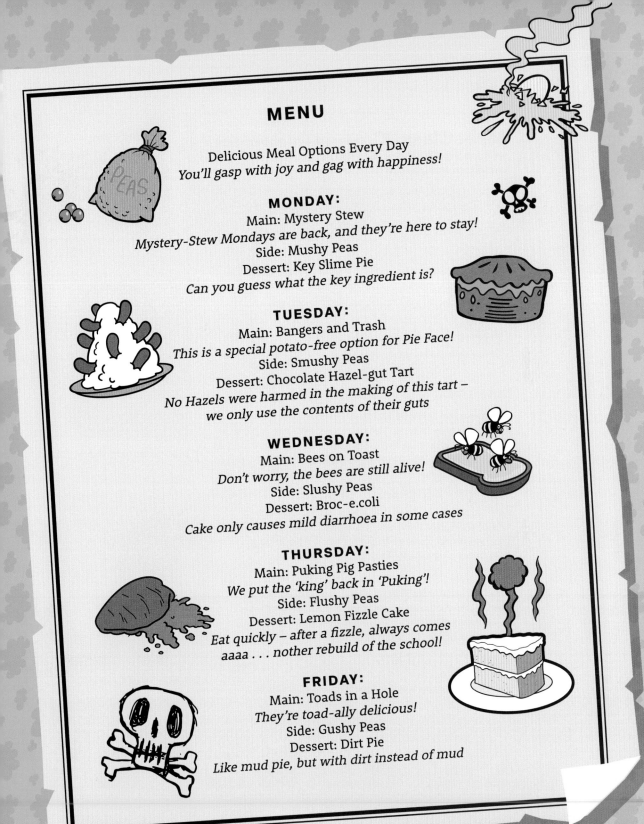

MENU

Delicious Meal Options Every Day
You'll gasp with joy and gag with happiness!

MONDAY:
Main: Mystery Stew
Mystery-Stew Mondays are back, and they're here to stay!
Side: Mushy Peas
Dessert: Key Slime Pie
Can you guess what the key ingredient is?

TUESDAY:
Main: Bangers and Trash
This is a special potato-free option for Pie Face!
Side: Smushy Peas
Dessert: Chocolate Hazel-gut Tart
*No Hazels were harmed in the making of this tart –
we only use the contents of their guts*

WEDNESDAY:
Main: Bees on Toast
Don't worry, the bees are still alive!
Side: Slushy Peas
Dessert: Broc-e.coli
Cake only causes mild diarrhoea in some cases

THURSDAY:
Main: Puking Pig Pasties
We put the 'king' back in 'Puking'!
Side: Flushy Peas
Dessert: Lemon Fizzle Cake
*Eat quickly – after a fizzle, always comes
aaaa . . . nother rebuild of the school!*

FRIDAY:
Main: Toads in a Hole
They're toad-ally delicious!
Side: Gushy Peas
Dessert: Dirt Pie
Like mud pie, but with dirt instead of mud

Meet Class 3C, the most well-known class at Bash Street School with the highest number of incidents reported to the headmaster's office . . .

Email Message ✉ ✎ ✈ 🗑

To: MrTesty@BeanotownSchoolInspector.com

From: E.Creecher@BashStreetSchool.com

Subject: From the desk of Mrs Edna Creecher, Bash Street School Headmaster

Dear Mr Testy,

Following the episode last month, which henceforth shall be known only as 'the mango-smoothie explosion', I can assure you that the culprits have been identified as the students in 3C, and they will receive the appropriate punishment. They will not be mango-ing anywhere until the walls are smooth-ie and sparkling clean.

I am also sorry to hear that you are still finding wee bits of mango juice in your only pair of pants. Should you be unable to clean them properly, I hope your search for a new pair of pants will be fruitful.

Rest assured that I have also spoken with their teacher, Miss Inika Mistry, about keeping a better eye on her students when they are performing 'health-food-based science experiments'. Let's not speak of this incident again.

Yours,
Mrs Edna Creecher
Headteacher and former East Kilbride Girl Guide

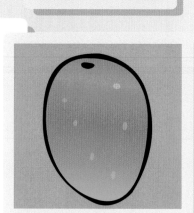

Mango before the incident

Miss Mistry of Class 3C

Email Message

To: E.Creecher@BashStreetSchool.com

From: I.MistryClass3C@BashStreetSchool.com

Subject: From the desk of Miss Mistry, 3C

Dear Mrs Creecher,

My students and I apologise for the small mess in the hallway following 'the mango-smoothie explosion'. As you know, we have been studying sustainable food sources, and one student's invention – a self-propelling hover-blender that scoops up hard-to-reach fruit and mixes it into healthy fruit-based drinks – was really quite brilliant, even if the prototype isn't quite ready. Rubidium Von Screwtop promises to do all further tests in her father's laboratory and not in the classroom.

Now that we have cleaned it up (using an eco-friendly soap recommended by another student, Maria Vittoria), we are moving on to a new lesson – the solar system. I have a hands-on experiment in mind, but I will planet carefully to avoid further fruit-based explosions. As always, I will continue to make sure Bash Street School is a fun place for creative, curious and energetic kids. My students this year are some of the smartest, most creative pupils I've ever taught.

Warmly,
Miss Inika Mistry

Rubidium Von Screwtop, inventor extraordinaire

Hover-blender explodes

INTERNAL SCHOOL NEWS BULLETIN

New yearbooks have been printed, but entries seem to have been amended by some of the pupils . . .

Miss Mistry is cool!

Miss Mistry was once a pupil at Bash Street School, which makes her a Bash Street Kid (once a Bash Street Kid, always a Bash Street Kid). Today she teaches Class 3C maths, science, reading, art . . . and, most importantly, she coaches the Bash Street's Super Epic Turbo Cricket team.

Full Name: Inika Mistry

Age: You can't ask a teacher how old they are!

Motto: 'My job is to help you all to become the best you can be.'

Likes: Teaching, crafting, cooking

Dislikes: Being forced to deal with too many regulations

Super skill: Ability to teach her students without turning them into little robots

THE ONLY TEACHER I'VE EVER NOT REALLY, REALLY DISLIKED!

VOTED BY HER STUDENTS
The coolest teacher at Bash Street School!

FAMILIAR FACES

Dennis Menace RULES!

VOTED BY HIS CLASSMATES
Most likely to: Fill the school bathroom soap dispensers with maple syrup.

Walter Brown

VOTED BY HIS CLASSMATES
Most likely to: Get his father to pay for an author to re-write this book, so it's all about him (with no mention of losers like Dennis).

Minnie Makepeace

VOTED BY ~~HER CLASSMATES~~ HERSELF
Most likely to: Win an award (and cash prize) for being the cleverest person in Beanotown, nay, the world!

Roger Dawson

VOTED BY HIS CLASSMATES
Most likely to: Never win a 'Most Likely Award' because he's so unpredictable, you can never guess where his dodges will take him!

Pie Face

Pie Face loves one food more than any other in the world. Can you guess which food? (Hint: It's not Brussel sprouts!) He is kind and funny, and loves to make people happy.

Full name: Peter Shepherd

Age: 10

Motto: 'There's nothing you can't put in a pie!'

Best friends: Dennis, Paul the potato

Likes: Eating, playing music, taking his pet potato to the park

Dislikes: Soggy bottoms, maths

Super skill: The ability to tell what filling is in a pie just by looking at it!

BEST MATE + FAVOURITE 'TUBER

Paul the potato

PIES! PIES! PIES!

VOTED BY HIS CLASSMATES
Most likely to: Discover a plant that grows pies!

Rubi ROCKS!

WHEELCHAIR STUNT EXPERT

Some people just about understand science, and others know their holey colanders from their hadron colliders. Rubi is part of the second group – she is super-smart and she loves doing experiments and inventing new gadgets.

Full name: Rubidium Von Screwtop

Age: 10

Motto: 'I have the answer!'

Best friends: Dennis, JJ, Pie Face

Likes: Science experiments, wheelchair stunts, adventures, telling jokes

Dislikes: Bullies, being late

Super skill: The ability to add built-in Wi-Fi and a mini fridge to any invention (her latest chair, laughing lava lamps, boomeranged frisbees – you name it!)

VOTED BY HER CLASSMATES
Most likely to: Create a mutant life form.

Billy Whizz

If you see a red blur speeding past you faster than you can blink, that's probably Billy Whizz. You'll recognise him if he slows down, but don't hold your breath. When he first started running, he went so fast that his nappy began to smoke! And that was when he was just two, when he took things a bit more slowly.

Full name: ~~Billiam Whizziam~~ (just kidding!) Billy Whizz

Age: 10

Top speed: *Ridiculously fast*

Motto: 'Can't stop!'

Best friends: Minnie, Dennis, Roger

Likes: PE class, athletics, relay races

Dislikes: Waiting, walking, strolling, just taking your time

Super skill: Always the first person to get anywhere

He's a TOP S-KID!

VOTED BY HIS CLASSMATES
Most likely to: Run so fast that they actually travel backwards in time!

Dangerous Dan

Dan is a ~~highly trained secret agent who works tirelessly to protect the people of Beanotown from the nefarious schemes of S.M.I.R.K. the Secret Ministry of Intelligent Rotters Komittee~~ regular boy who lives in Beanotown and just happens to wear a tuxedo that's totally not full of spy gadgets. Nothing suspicious about that.

Full name: Dan Badu (but tell NO ONE!)

Age: 00-10

Motto: 'I've got a plot to foil!'

Best friends: ~~Agent Q~~ Dennis, Mandi, Rubi

Likes: ~~Foiling enemy agents,~~ football, breaking secret codes, being normal

Dislikes: Changing his socks (what's wrong with the ones he has on right now?)

Super skill: ~~Fighting evil schemes to save the world.~~ Being an ordinary guy who has a nice smile

[TOP SECRET]

VOTED BY HIS CLASSMATES
Most likely to: Use a grappling hook disguised as a rubber to sneak in late to school.

Angel Face

Angel Face is the class detective and runs her own Investigating Agency. She can solve any case . . . for a price. If you want her to solve your crime, you'll need to give her something that tastes sublime.

Full name: Angel De Testa

Age: 10

Motto: 'What's in it for me? Erm, I mean . . . how can I help?'

Best friend: Jenny

Likes: Biscuits, brownies, ice cream, cake, cookies, doughnuts . . . any baked good, really

Dislikes: People who ask for free favours

Super skill: Can solve any case

VOTED BY HER CLASSMATES
Most likely to: Solve a massive crime, but refuse to hand over the evidence to the police until she gets her payment of an ice cream sundae.

Bertie

Bertie would call himself Walter Brown's best friend. Walter, on the other hand, would probably say that Bertie is a useful minion to have around and follow his orders. Then Bertie would agree with what Walter said – he usually does.

Full name: Bertie Blenkinsop

Age: 10

Motto: 'Yes, Walter. That's an epic idea, Walter.'

Best friend: Walter

Likes: Money, snakes, anything that Walter Brown likes

Dislikes: Riding horses, hard work

Super skill: Tale-telling, whether or not it's actually true (does it really matter if it's good gossip?)

Walter is awesome!

VOTED BY HIS CLASSMATES
Most likely to: Follow Walter onto a spooky clifftop and then get left behind when there's only one parachute to escape with.

JJ Catch me if you can!

JJ is confident, active and fearless. She loves the spooky and unexplained, and sports (football, BMX, gymnastics, Blamjitsu, and drone-dangling heli-skateboarding, to name a few . . .), especially if she's on the winning team. She'll also do anything for her friends!

Full name: Jem Jones

Age: 10

Motto: 'Give it your all!'

Best friends: Rubi, Dennis, Pie Face

Likes: Sports, drumming, helping people, ghosts

Dislikes: Losing, laziness, bullies

Super skill: Can understand what Rubi is saying, even when Rubi uses her most complex scientific language. If Rubi asks for an aerodynamic sphere for metatarsal-based competition, JJ knows to bring her a football!

VOTED BY HER CLASSMATES
Most likely to: Challenge her four older brothers to a race across Beanotown . . . and beat them all!

Vito Eco-Warrior

SAVE THE PLANET!

Vito is fearless and energetic. She's also the greenest person you'll meet in Beanotown. (She's not actually green – except when she accidentally takes a bite of the Olives' mystery stew – she just cares a lot about keeping the Earth clean!)

Full name: Maria Vittoria

Age: 10

Motto: 'Superheroes won't save the planet – we have to do it ourselves!'

Best friends: Rubi, Dennis

Likes: Animals and wildlife, playing games

Dislikes: Litterbugs, plant-stompers

Super skill: Knowing if someone hasn't recycled just by looking at them

VOTED BY HER CLASSMATES
Most likely to: Catch Wilbur Brown littering – and make him go back to put it in the bin!

Three Questions for The Dinmakers

All That Jazz MAGAZINE

The Dinmakers is the fastest and loudest rock band in Beanotown. They are loud, energetic and raw. Oh, did we mention that they're loud?

By Burt Crowbrain

Like whoa! I was lucky enough to jam with Beanotown's brassiest rock band last night, and it was a clangour for sure! Lead guitarist Dennis and drummer 'JJ-All-the-Way' answered my questions:

Burt: What's your newest song?

Dennis: It's called Kerrang-a-tang! and it's inspired by the sounds that come from the orangutan enclosure at Beanotown Zoo during feeding time.

Burt: It sounds like a howler! What other places do you get your inspiration from?

JJ: Oh, anything that moves quickly. That's why we're the fastest band in Beantown.

Dennis: And we're also the LOUDEST band in Beanotown!

Burt: And what would you say your secret for success is?

Dennis: It's all about my dancing skills.

JJ: Don't be silly, Dennis. It's all our hard work! We spend loads of time practising out in Beanotown Woods and all of us – Rubi, Pie Face, Gnasher, Dennis and I – work together. Like that time Pie Face wrote a new song about his pet potato, Paul, but I came up with the drum solo and Rubi was the tech genius behind the electric beats. We're a great team.

Dennis: But I've got funky moves.

Meet Class 2B, otherwise known as The Bash Street Kids. This is a tight-knit group that gives Dennis, Minnie and their friends a run for their money at pranking!

From the desk of Mr Walter Winterbottom, Teacher, 2B

To: Mrs Creecher, Headteacher

Dear Mrs Creecher,

I was really inspired by your talk last week about the first 200 of the 923 school rules. You recited them so clearly and diligently, and I particularly liked when you elaborated on the rule about always listening to your teacher. As you know, I have devoted my life to passing knowledge on to the next generation. If my class would just listen a bit more, I could keep educating and educating and educating them!

If it's not too much to ask, would you have time to discuss the remaining 723 school rules? I eagerly await your answer. In the meantime, I'm off to take my teacher-strength painkillers to get me through this soon 2B headache!

Yours,

W.Winterbottom

Mr Teacher
(Walter Winterbottom)

WARNING UNRULY KIDS!

102

BSK - AKA The Bash Street Kids

Mahira:
Bad news, Teacher has a plan to make us listen to him more. 🎤🎓😀

Danny:
What?! But all he ever says is blah-blah-stuff-blah-blah-learning. There are much more interesting things I could be doing. Like daydreaming about digging for Greenbeard's buried pirate treasure on Beanotown Beach . . . 💰💎

Sidney:
What do we do? Harsha, has the joke shop got any wide-awake glasses left? 👓

Harsha:
They're sold out! Besides, we need something else instead – like ear plugs.

Smiffy:
U need ears from Plug? 🔊 I bet Plug will be happy to lend u his ears. 👂👂

Plug:
I do have the perfect ears! 😃

Wilfrid:
I'm going to pull up my jumper to cover my ears more. Then I won't have to listen.

Scotty:
And I'll wrap my tie around my head.

Stevie:
I have a plan. We'll have to distract Teacher somehow. 💩

Toots:
No, I'll tell u what we're going to do. Every time Teacher says something, someone says, 'Can u speak up? I can't hear u.' He'll have to get louder and louder and pretty soon he'll lose his voice from shouting, and we won't have to listen for the rest of the week! 😃

DANNY

Full Name: Danny Morgan

Age: 10

Address: 3rd Floor, Bash Street Towers

Role: Class 2B student, leader of the Bash Street Kids, aspiring pirate

Known associates: Bones the dog

Features: Skull-and-crossbones jumper, red-and-black striped hat

Wanted for:

• Sleeping through class

• Singing pirate shanties when he should be studying

• Using his telescope to spy on neighbours

BONES THE DOG →

Full Name: Mandira Sharma

Age: 9

Address: 22 Sutherland Crescent

Role: Class 2B student, planner

Known associates: Minnie, Rubi, Dangerous Dan

Features: Worried but determined expression

Wanted for:

• Over-planning pranks, to the point where she talks herself out of them

• Bringing her pet rabbit Milo into school because she was worried he would be lonely at home

• Letting Milo eat Mr Teacher's coat because it makes him happy (the rabbit, not Mr Teacher!)

MANDI

TOOTS

PEEPS THE DOG

Full Name: Kate Pye

Age: 9

Address: Top Floor, Bash Street Towers

Role: Class 2B student, actual leader of the Bash Street Kids

Known associates: Twin brother Sidney, Peeps the dog

Features: Red hairbow, blue-and-black striped jumper

Wanted for:

- Using the bow in her hair as a catapult to knock coffee off Mr Teacher's desk

- Holding up traffic when performing street dancing

- Making a loud tooting noise – that's where she got her nickname!

SIDNEY

WIGGY THE DOG

Full Name: Sidney Pye

Age: 9

Address: Top Floor, Bash Street Towers

Role: 2B student, animal-lover

Known associates: Patrick the pigeon

Features: Unruly black hair, blue-and-black striped jumper

Wanted for:

- Replacing Mr Teacher's breath mints with dog kibble

- Training his pet pigeon on public property, leaving behind a trail of sticky pigeon poo

- Frightening residents of Bash Street Towers with his collection of lizards, birds, creepy-crawlies and Wiggy the dog

SCOTTY

BLOTTY THE DOG →

Full Name: James Scott Cameron

Age: 10

Address: 8th Floor, Bash Street Towers

Role: Class 2B student, prankster

Known associates: Blotty the Dog

Features: Small for his age, spots on his face, super-long tie

Wanted for:

- Pranking people who don't like having fun, such as filling Cuthbert Cringeworthy's briefcase with 89 spotty bouncy balls

- Tripping people up with his extra-long school tie

- Starting loud arguments with inanimate objects such as lampposts and pickle jars

Full Name: Wilfrid Bramble

Age: 9

Address: 7th floor, Bash Street Towers

Role: Class 2B student, magician

Known associates: Manfrid the dog, Irma the tortoise

Features: Baggy green jumper that nearly hides his face

Wanted for:

- Making Mr Teacher's assignment book disappear

- Making everyone else's homework disappear

- Making himself disappear to get out of class

WILFRID

MANFRID THE DOG →

MAHIRA

Full Name: Mahira Salim

Age: (Number) 10

Address: 1st Floor, Bash Street Towers

Role: Class 2B student, football superstar, mathlete

Known associates: The entire Beanotown Untied women's football team, JJ

Features: Football kit with goal-den boots, pink headband

Wanted for:
• Breaking a keepie-uppie world record with the class globe in the middle of a geography lesson

• Correcting Mr Teacher's maths in front of the class

• Practising football under the table while doing her school work

CUTHBERT

Full Name: Cuthbert Creeply Cringeworthy

Age: 10

Address: 28A Acacia Road

Role: Class 2B student, teacher's pet

Known associates: Humphrey the Shetland pony, Mr Teacher (he wishes!)

Features: Glasses, red blazer, blue cap

Wanted for:
Oh this is tricky as I never break any of the rules. I guess if I'm guilty of anything, it would be making the rest of the class look dull in comparison to my brilliance, or of being so amazing that Mr Teacher doesn't have enough awards to give me.

eaoaoaoaoaoaoaoaoaoaooao

Full Name: Percival Proudfoot Plugseley

Age: 9

Address: 32 Gasworks Road

Role: Dangerously attractive student

Known associates: Glug the fish, Pug the dog

Features: His 'amazingly good looks'

Wanted for:

- Smashing mirrors all over Beanotown just by winking at them

- Causing residents of Beanotown to start to crying when they see his beauty

- Knocking down a wall at the Beanotown Museum by hanging up too many portraits of himself (in order to make the museum 'more beautiful')

PLUG

PUG THE DOG

Full Name: Herbert Henry Hoover

Age: 9

Address: 2nd Floor, Bash Street Towers

Role: Class 2B student, prankster

Known associates: Plug, Enry the dog

Features: Thick glasses

Wanted for:

- Toppling over Veg Dwight's carefully built tower of 946 tomatoes at Rocket Man Vegetarian Delicatessen

- Painting double yellow lines in the teacher's car park, making them all late to class

- Swapping the PUSH and PULL signs on all the school doors, making Mr Teacher EVEN LATER!

ERBERT

ENRY THE DOG

FREDDY

TUBBY THE DOG

Full Name: Frederick Brown

Age: 9

Address: 5th floor, Bash Street Towers

Role: Class 2B student, gymnast, musical theatre enthusiast

Known associates: Tubby the dog

Features: Red jacket, yellow vest

Wanted for:

• Using an epic straddle tuck-jump turn to knock over Mr Teacher's desk and then blame it on Cuthbert Cringeworthy

• Singing the entire soundtrack of Matilda the Musical mid-class and blaming it on Cuthbert Cringeworthy

• Arriving late for school . . . and blaming it on Cuthbert Cringeworthy

STEVIE

Full Name: Stephen Super Star

Age: 10 (out of 10!)

Address: 17 Greenbelt Drive

Role: Class 2B student, you-hoober

Known associates: Plug, Miss Mistry

Features: Phone constantly filming on selfie mode

Wanted for:

• Posting a video of Mr Teacher farting in the teacher's lounge on You-Hoo

• Chasing Butch Butcher for an exclusive interview, thinking he was the real Elvis Presley

• Borrowing Taylor Rift's taxidermy cat for show and tell (without asking his mum)

Full Name: Khadija Raad

Age: 9

Address: 10 Acacia Road

Role: Class 2B student, creative rebel

Known associates: Dennis, Rubi

Features: Purple hijab with butterfly, art pack on her back

Wanted for:

- Creating posters exposing the real ingredients in the school dinners

- Drawing a spider on Mr Teacher's desk that makes him squeal

- Distracting the class with funny illustrations on the windows when they steam up

SKETCH KHAD

Full Name: Aristotle Smith

Age: 10

Address: 11th Floor, Bash Street Towers

Role: Class 2B student, sidekick to Danny's madcap schemes

Known associates: Kevin the pet pebble, Sniffy the dog

Features: Vacant expression, large front teeth

Wanted for:

- Thwarting teachers by acting so foolishly that it's really quite clever

- Causing mayhem after calling Sergeant Slipper to investigate a stranger in the house . . . which turned out to be just his own reflection in the mirror

- Tripping up people in the park while taking his pet pebble for a walk

SMIFFY

SNIFFY THE DOG

JOKES & PRANKS

Hey Toots!
I bet my jokes can make you laugh more than Spotty's fart whistle.

Why did the broomstick get in trouble with Mr Teacher?

Because it kept sweeping in class!

Why did the giraffe get in trouble with Mr Teacher?

Because it had its head up in the clouds!

Why did the echo get in trouble with Mr Teacher?

Because it kept answering back!

Why did Toots get sent out of the classroom?

Because her bottom wouldn't stop tooting in class!

(Oh wait ... the last one isn't a joke, it's a true story!)

From, Sidney

Hi, Bro!
Har har. I bet my top pranks will make you giggle even more – because they are jokes AND true stories!

Do you remember when I tied Cuthbert's laces together?

It did knot end well for him!

What happened when I stole Cuthbert's maths book and hid it in Danny's bag?

The extra problems were weighing Danny down.

What happened when I sneaked a push-pin onto Mr Teacher's chair?

He said, 'Oh dear, my chair is under a tack!'

Why is my annoying brother Sidney like one of Wilfrid's sneaky farts?

Because you never know when they might be expelled!

From, Toots

111

BEANOTOWN ODDITIES

Up until now, you're probably thinking that Beanotown sounds like an unusual sort of place. Maybe just a teensy-weensy bit different from where you are right now. Ha! You don't know the half of it! In this final chapter, you'll learn even more of the secrets and oddities that surround Beanotown. Even the residents have given up trying to understand them all!

This looks like a normal island in a normal duck pond, right?

WRONG! Duck Island is bonkers!

There are mysterious and huge pyramids. Who built them? Nobody knows!

Did you know Beanotown was founded by Vikings in 801 CE? There is a lost tribe of Vikings still living on Duck Island!

Steer well clear of the meat-eating plants. They're big enough to swallow you whole!

BHS The Beanotown History Society

WE'RE LIKING VIKINGS!

By Doug Deeper (BHS Archeological Expert)

History has been around for, well, for a long time – and history in Beanotown is no exception. The first known residents in the area that is now known as Beanotown were a tribe of people who were said to look strangely like Walter and Wilbur Brown. This was a very dull tribe that didn't accomplish much other than yelling at other tribes to keep off their lawns.

That all changed when the Vikings arrived in 801 CE. A battle broke out over a loo roll and a few magic beans. The Vikings were victorious, and they turned Beanotown into the awesome place it is today. They built the original Beanotown town centre, including the secret tunnels that connect the caves under the town. They also brought these funny-looking helmets into fashion!

An ~~Hysterical~~ Historical Discovery by Professor Von Screwtop

Fascinating! My research into the space-time continu-bum has revealed something utterly unexpected. By doing complex maths problems and by analysing a preserved specimen of Viking poo, I have found irrefutable proof that Dennis Menace and his canine companion Gnasher must have somehow travelled back to the era of Beanotown's Vikings. Who knows what misadventures that dynamic duo got up to over 1,000 years ago!

But enough with time travel. I've already started work on my next invention: a SLIME-travel machine...

Viking Poo

BEANOTOWN'S SECRET TUNNELS

One of Beanotown's worst-kept secrets is the maze of tunnels beneath Bash Street School. If you find your way through the mysterious old trapdoor in the basement, you'll be following in the footsteps of generations of brave kids who have escaped from boring lessons and strict teachers.

WHAT SHOULD I DO IN THE CREEPY SCHOOL TUNNEL?

I survived once, but what if I end up there again? Here's a flowchart to help me plan what might happen. I'm sure you'll C the clear answer too . . .

MANDI SHARMA

1 As you walk down the dark, creepy, slimy tunnel, you notice the skull of an ancient T-rex, and its eyes are glowing! Should you:

A Offer it some eye drops. Its eyes are probably itchy and uncomfortable from 1,000 years of dust.

B Challenge the skull to a staring contest. Whoever blinks first loses an eye.

C Run!

2 The walls are lined with ancient carvings. You stop to read one out loud, and then realise you've accidentally released a terrible curse upon all of Beanotown. Should you:

A Quickly find the feather of a pigeon and the poo of a dove to bind the curse back into the ancient carving.

B Tell the curse your funniest jokes – even a curse can't resist a good chuckle, and it might stick around to hear more rather than torment the residents of Beanotown.

C Run!

JOKE BOOK

3 You continue past a pile of hungry, angry crocodiles. They have big, sharp teeth and terrible breath, but luckily they're fast asleep ... oops, you just stepped on the big one's tail and now they've all woken up and want to eat you. Should you:

A Throw the spikiest rocks at the crocs.

B Throw your smelliest socks at the crocs.

C Run!

4 You sneeze (must be all the Viking dust). You reach up to pick the tiniest bogey from your nose and flick it away. Um, that was snot a good idea. The tiny bogey bumps into a tiny pebble, which nudges a bigger stone, which tips into a giant rock, which dislodges a MASSIVE boulder that's now rolling at 200mph straight towards you. Should you:

A Kick it like you're playing for Beanotown Untied and score the best-ever own goal.

B Using only your toenails, dig a channel going in the other direction to divert the boulder.

C Run!

5 You're nearly out of the tunnels near the beach at Beanotown-on-Sea ... but something's rotten. Dennis has just farted. Should you:

A Hold your breath.

B Fart louder than him.

C Run!

PONG!

WORM'S EYE VIEW OF THE SECRET TUNNELS

HORRIBLE HALL

TAKE OUR ADVICE

and steer well clear of the ruins of
Horrible Hall during your visit. Long, long, LONG ago, Horrible Hall was the school in Beanotown.
Ever since it was mysteriously destroyed, a headless headmaster has haunted its ruins.

HAUNTED! KEEP OUT!

EVEN THE TOURIST GUIDE IS A G-G-GHOST.

And once you're in there, lost among the long
corridors, it's hard to find the way out. There
are ghost teachers everywhere you turn.

SOMETIMES THE HALL ITSELF VANISHES!

And some of the Beanotown residents wish
it would stay that way!

DENNIS'S TIME TRAVEL APP

LOCATION # TOWN HALL CLOCK TOWER

Another mind-blowing secret is hidden in the clock tower on the top of the town hall. Sure, it can tell the time and make lots of dooooong noises at midday, but it's also home to a time machine. There are instructions somewhere, although no one has ever read them. Happy travels anyways!

 **400 BCE**

The Greek **Dionysius the Elder of Syracuse** invented the first-ever catapult. This man is my hero. If you see him, give him a big high five from me!

 1066

Travel back to see **William the Conqueror** defeat Harold at the Battle of Hastings. Lots of exciting sword fighting and archery! This was also the year that Lord Phillius Butt broke the world record for the longest fart (14 hours, 7 minutes).

1596

This was when **William Shakespeare** wrote his famous play Romeo and Juliet. Please, for all the young kids out there who will be forced to study this apparently romantic script for years to come, STOP HIM!

1687

If you go to this year, you'll learn another secret. **Sir Isaac Newton** discovered gravity . . . but if you think you know what fell on his head, you're apple-solutely wrong. It wasn't an apple that hit him – it was a banana cream pie. I should know – I threw it!

1876

Visit this year to see **Alexander Graham Bell** invent the telephone. You can also see him trying to text his mates the poo emoji, but it didn't work because his mates didn't have signal yet.

WHERE DO YOU WANT TO GO?

DUCK ISLAND

No visit to Beanotown is complete without seeing the famous Duck Island. The tiny, innocent-looking island in the middle of Beanotown Park's duck pond is bigger on the inside, and if you set so much as a toenail on it, you're likely to face a Jurassic-sized problem.

The reason for Duck Island's mysteries is an asteroid that hit it 65 million years ago. It created a compression field, squashing everything on the island to a fraction of its size. There is a machine around the asteroid that keeps it small. If it ever broke, Duck Island would spread out across the country. Eek!

ANGEL FACE
Private Detective
No job is too big!

Angel Face   Jenny

There's a lot going on at Duck Island!

ANGEL FACE'S CASEBOOK

Tuesday night, 5:24pm

Heard a rumour from Dennis's gran (of all people!) about dinosaurs roaming around Duck Island. Jenny says we should check it out and maybe we'll find a dinosaur bone or two. I bet Beanotown Museum would pay big bucks for that!

Tuesday night, 6:58pm

Arrived at the park via Beanotown Station. It was just starting to get dark, but Jenny had her torch. We waited about a stone's throw from Duck Island.

Tuesday night, 7:05pm

Ok, that was weird! I could have sworn I saw a gigantic dog that looks just like Dennis's pet. How come he keeps showing up everywhere? Is this someone's conspiracy to clone Gnasher, so that he can take over the world? (Note to self: Maybe I could do that?)

Tuesday night, 7:21pm

Jenny says to be brave and get a bit closer, so we've taken a few extra steps. Now we can see eerie shadows of something that's either a person with two horns on their head, or someone wearing a silly Viking hat.

Tuesday night, 7:43pm

Is that a volcano erupting? That's definitely a volcano. Or a giant bear who ate too many lava-coloured berries and is throwing up.

Tuesday night, 7:55pm

Are you kidding? My dad just texted to say I have to be home for bedtime. Maybe the real conspiracy is that he wants to be the one to find dinosaur bones to sell to the museum. I dino for sure, but it's pretty suspicious!

LAKE MESS

From a distance, Lake Mess looks like a tranquil beauty spot. And from a distance is probably the best way to enjoy it! If you're looking for time outside and a few hours of peaceful fishing, then this is not the place for you.

Up close, this place is ... well ... a bit of a mess. No one knows for certain what secrets might be lurking inside!

DANGER!

Wild swimming is not advisable here!

ANGEL FACE'S CASEBOOK

Wednesday afternoon, 12:30pm

A new case for Angel Face! Roger the Dodger lost his fishing rod at Lake Mess when he went fishing with his dad. (Roger doesn't like fishing, but his dad's going to take his pocket money until he has enough to replace the rod). Roger will pay us two packs of his jammy biscuits if Jenny and I can track it down. That's one pack for me, and the other one . . . also for me. We'll go after school.

Wednesday afternoon, 12:38pm

Roger mentioned something about creepy, muddy footprints. I tried to get more information out of him, but he kept dodging my questions.

Wednesday afternoon, 3:45pm

Arrived at Lake Mess and just walked past the warning signs. Ha! Who pays attention to those?

Wednesday afternoon, 3:46pm

I think I see Roger's fishing rod! My detective skills have already paid off. That's 24 biscuits for just a few minutes of work . . .

Wednesday afternoon, 3:47pm

Ok, now that we're closer, I can see it's just a rusty bicycle.

Wednesday afternoon, 3:51pm

Ooh, is that it?

Wednesday afternoon, 3:52pm

No, it's someone's unwanted wellies.

Wednesday afternoon, 3:58pm

What was that terrifying scream?

Wednesday afternoon, 3:59pm

Jenny, are you trying to prank me? That's not funny.

Wednesday afternoon, 4:01pm

It's still shrieking . . . it's coming from the water . . . are those tentacles reaching up, coming right at me, trying to grab my ankles?

Wednesday afternoon, 4:01pm

Forget this - Roger can find his own fishing rod! I'm just going to visit Dennis's gran and she'll probably share one of her posh biscuits with me and Jenny. In fact, we'd better run as fast as we can - not because we're scared, of course . . . we just need to get there before she's out of biscuits!

If you're out in Beanotown Woods, you might stumble across

DENNIS'S DEN

It's huge and epic and fun . . . but no groan-ups are allowed, sorry (not sorry).

How to Build the Perfect Den in the Woods

If you need somewhere to hang out and plan your next prank away from those pesky groan-ups, you should build a den! Here are the things you will need.

TRAPDOOR

Every den needs a secret trapdoor! Mine is hidden beneath the mess of cables behind the TV. No one ever looks too closely because a tangle of cables is one of the scariest things out there!

BEANO

SOLAR PANEL

Vito told me to put this in. Apparently, it captures sunlight and makes my den more eco-friendly. Who needs sunlight though — I'm already so radiant!

A FRIDGE

A place for all your snacks. You should never prank on an empty stomach (Just ask Pie Face — he was so hungry, he couldn't resist trying the chilli-pie lolly himself. He didn't talk about it much afterwards... because his tongue was too swollen to speak!).

MISCHIEF DISPENSER

I recommend at least four different catapults, three peashooters, two squishy tomatoes and a partridge in a pear tree (Just kidding about the last one. Sort of. Come to think about it, rotten pears are also good for making splats, and you could train the partridge to poo on Walter's new shoes!).

EXIT

SUPER-SLIDE RAMP

Why leave on foot when you can slide down? Wheee! Plus, we needed a way for Rubi to get in, so it's a win-win!

INJURY HILL

Injury Hill is the steepest street in Beanotown. It's so steep that it's physically impossible to stand upright on it. Just ask Professor Von Screwtop. He's always up for explaining the science of gravity. Injury Hill is great for sledding down though!

GRAVITY AND STEEP SLOPES CAN BE DANGEROUS!

WOO HOO!

VERY STEEP!

CRASH!

What I Did Last Weekend
by Betty Bhu, Class 1A

My best friend Yeti and I went sledding down Injury Hill. Dennis built a giant snow slide just outside Mr Chop's Barbershop. The slide was steeper than Mount Everest, which is a mountain in Nepal near where I grew up before I came to Beanotown. My grandma still lives there. Her village gets enough snow to make ten million snowballs!

Yeti came from Nepal too. Then they lived on the slopes of Mount Beano for a while. Yeti loves the cold. In the summer, they have to eat lots of ice cream to stay cool. I have to eat ice cream too, because Yeti would feel lonely if I didn't. In the winter, we have to eat even more ice cream, because the ice cream would feel lonely if we ignored it just because it's very cold outside.

I like to slide as fast as I can down Injury Hill. Sometimes I feel like I'm flying! Luckily, I usually land in a big pile of snow, which is nice and soft. Otherwise, Yeti catches me!

Great report, Betty. And great imagination! I love how you use make believe to create a snow monster to tell a great story!

Betty Bhu has a secret. A BIG secret. She doesn't actually have a cousin called Agnes. You're probably thinking WHAT?! So, who's the large girl with pigtails you often see alongside Betty? Well, believe it or not, that's not a girl at all but Biggy Smells, or Yeti as Betty calls them. If you're thinking, but yetis don't exist, then you must be a grown-up - they all think Biggy is just someone dressed up as a yeti to make the library more fun. Adults have such silly imaginations!

YETI

BETTY

Full name: Betty Bhu
Age: 7
Class: 1A
Address: 8 Bagge-shott Wynde
Likes: Dressing up, ballet, glitter, Yeti
Dislikes: Not getting her own way
Biggest fear: Her dad finding out about Yeti
Best quality: Caring
Top skills: Giving orders, taking control
Favourite food: Ice cream

Also known as: Biggy Smells or Cousin Agnes
Age: Nobody knows - could be anything from 7 to 700
Class: 1A
Address: A large hiding place in Betty's house
Job: Librarian
Likes: Betty, disguises
Dislikes: Being too hot
Biggest fear: Yeti hunters
Best quality: Good learner
Top skills: Strength, disguising themself
Favourite food: Cake

BEANOTOWN ALLOTMENTS

What's that? We're nearly at the end of this guidebook and we haven't even covered the Beanotown Allotments yet? Well, I do beg your garden! There's no fresher or greener place in Beanotown, and you better be-leaf it.

BEANO NEWS

ALLOT TO SHOUT ABOUT!

BY ANNE FINELY

Young Allotmenteer MARIA VITTORIA AKA VITO

Anne Finely from Beano News here, reporting on the action at Beanotown Allotments! The residents of Beanotown have managed to catch the gardening bug somehow. Here with me is Maria Vittoria to help me dig into it.

Anne: So what's the story, Vito? Why are children all across Beanotown suddenly trading in their pranks for plant pots?

Vito: I'm here because growing your own organic fruits and vegetables is a great way to help out the planet! My friends all have their own reasons too. Rubi is doing scientific experiments with new irrigation systems and Minnie wants to grow squishy tomatoes to throw at people.

Anne: My sources tell me someone was meddling with dangerous scientific chemicals to make a super-growth serum that could turn vegetables into evil, killer zombies.

Vito: That's an awful idea. Artificial chemicals are terrible for the bees and the trees, and also for us.

Anne: Ok, but let's just say it did happen and you found yourself face-to-face with an evil kung-fu beetroot whose leaves were on fire. Could you beat the beetroot in a fight?

Vito: Of course.

Anne: You grow, girl!

Artists impression of what chemically grown zombie veg could look like! (Not very nice at all!)

THE BUZZ

Calling all insects and garden molluscs! Are you feeling sluggish? Do you want a quiet place where everyone will stop bugging you? Come to Beanotown Allotments and stay in the Premium Bug Hotel! This brilli-ant new wooden box is filled with your favourite things: grass, twigs and some bark. It's pretty fly! Check us out on the web to book your room today.

'I shell be staying there!'
RUSTY SNAIL

WILDLIFE SPOTTER'S GUIDE

Beanotown's wildlife is a bit, erm, wilder than you might expect.

Here is a handy spotter's guide to tick off all the creatures you might see here:

SEWER CREATURES

Grasping beasties slither their slimy tentacles through Beanotown's drain covers, searching for scraps of food and tripping up passers-by as an added bonus.

BIRDS

Beanotown birds are as quirky and egg-centric as the people. You might see them sipping drinks as they fly along, or even wearing clothes.

MYSTERY CREATURES

Watch out for eerie eyes peering at you from inside small gaps and post-box slots. No one really knows what they are and no one expects to ever find out.

LAKE MESS MONSTER

This gargantuan beast lives in Lake Mess and is often heard but rarely seen.

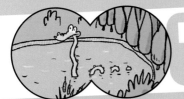

RODNEY THE RAM

Rodney provides the red wool for Dennis's and Minnie's beloved jumpers. He lives high up on Mount Beano among the snow and ice.

MR FROSTY

Mr Frosty, a 365-days-of-the-year living snowman, is happiest playing in the snow on Mount Beano.

Squelchy Things!

These wobbly, squishy little creatures live underneath Beanotown, but they regularly come up to the surface to laugh at people - especially people who have just been pranked! They were accidentally created by Professor Crackpott, and set free by Calamity James.

1

SQUELCH!

Super-rare strawberry-flavoured squelchy thing

2

Unkempt squelchy thing

3

Angry Viking squelchy thing

FACT: Human beings can't see squelchy things, but animals can! Rubi invented a squelchy-translator so she could communicate with them!

4

Scrawny squelchy thing

5

GUZZLE! GORGE! STUFF!

CRAM!

Happy sausage-nabbing squelchy thing

6

BOING!

BOING! SQUELCH!

Bouncy squelchy thing

Science Report

by **CALAMITY JAMES**
(with help from **RUBI VON SCREWTOP**)

AND I'M HERE IN CASE JAMES TRIES TO SET OFF ANOTHER EXPLOSION IN THE SCIENCE LAB.

REMEMBER THOSE SQUELCHY THINGS THAT I ACCIDENTALLY SET FREE? (IT WAS REALLY UNLUCKY HOW THAT HAPPENED!) I'M GOING TO INTERVIEW THEM FOR MY SCIENCE REPORT!

CALAMITY JAMES: That was an accident! I didn't know that Dennis's itching powder had expired and would react so badly when I spilled my fizzy cola on it . . .

1 Hehehe, Squelch!

CJ: So, Professor Crackpott says that you're the fastest-breeding life form on Earth. Is that correct?

6 Boing! Squelch! Boing!

RUBI: I think that means 'yes'.

CJ: How many of you are there now?

5 Gurgle! Blorg!

RUBI: I don't think the Squelchy Things can count.

CJ: I love to count to 13. Some say it's unlucky, but they'd be wro—

RUBI: James! You almost knocked over the beaker. Be careful . . .

CJ: Oops! Ok, Squelchy Things: What's your favourite joke? Mine is: What do you get when the king and queen trip over a cable, crash into a table full of test tubes whose contents mix and start to bubble and slime up?

2 Squeeeeeelch! Hahahahah!

RUBI: I know the answer - a royal mess!

CALAMITY JAMES'S BEDROOM! Can you spot where the Squelchy Things live?

The Numskulls

IT'S WHAT'S INSIDE THAT COUNTS!

SCIENCE FAIR PROJECT BY RUBI VON SCREWTOP

Until recently, it was believed that only Edd Ache had numskulls, but it has been recently discovered by Rubi Von Screwtop that everyone in Beanotown has tiny versions of themselves living inside their bodies. They help to make sure that bodies work the way they should. There are also Tumskulls (stomach department) and Bumskulls . . . but let's stop right there.

BRAINY
Brain Department

BLINKY
Eye Department

SNITCH
Nose Department

CRUNCHER
Mouth Department

RADAR
Ear Department

Using ba-nanotechnology, string theory and science, I've invented a

M.I.N.D. READER
(**M**arvellous **I**magination **N**eurotransmission **D**evice)

that projects the voices of your numskulls. Watch as I demonstrate by attaching it to Edd's head . . .

Wow, we're so smart! I can't think of anyone who is more cleverer than us!

And look at us in the mirror. I think this helmet could be the next big fashion thing! It's much cooler than that silly Viking hat Dennis wore once.

I'm putting on my music - we need a cool song playing. How about 'The Sound of Science'?

That's a terrible song, it's just someone smashing beakers together and shouting 'The beakers are ALIVEEEE with the sound of a reaction . . . FIIIIIIZZ!'. That song stinks!

If you like this machine as much as I do, put your money where your mouth is. Or put your money where my mouth is. Actually, just put some popcorn where my mouth is - popcorn tastes better.

What it looks like inside Edd Ache's head!

Brainy's Department

133

And now... THE BIG BEANOTOWN QUIZ!

One last thing before you leave – can you complete the quiz? Now is the chance to find out if you have been paying attention ... or have you been too busy making paper aeroplanes at the back of the class?

Only write in this book if you own it – you don't want to get on Biggy Smells' bad side for writing in a library book!

1

Who built the very first Beanotown?

- [ ] **A)** Dinosaurs
- [ ] **B)** Vikings
- [ ] **C)** Numskulls
- [ ] **D)** I. P. Daley

BEANO TOWN →

2

Where can you learn more about the history of Beanotown?

- [ ] **A)** Mount Beano
- [ ] **B)** Beanotown Police Office
- [ ] **C)** Beanotown Museum
- [ ] **D)** Just ask Gnasher the dog

THE HISTORY OF BEANOTOWN

3

Who is the mayor of Beanotown?

- [ ] **A)** A dog
- [ ] **B)** A cat
- [ ] **C)** A chimp
- [ ] **D)** Wilbur Brown

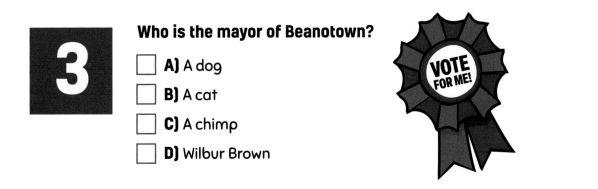

4

If you want to sound like a local, what should you say if someone scores a double goal in Super Epic Turbo Cricket?

- [ ] **A)** That was totally blam!
- [ ] **B)** Prithee tell me, dost thou knowest the rules to this jolly game?
- [ ] **C)** Has anyone caught the Golden Snitch yet?
- [ ] **D)** Who cares about Super Epic Turbo Cricket? I love homework!

5

Where does the Menace family live? (You need to know so you can avoid it!)

- [ ] **A)** 31 Sutherland Crescent
- [ ] **B)** 41 Bash Street Towers
- [ ] **C)** 51 Gasworks Road
- [ ] **D)** 61 Fartyourpantsoff Road

D. Menace
????????????
Beanotown

HOW ARE YOU GETTING ON? IT'S NOT OVER YET. MORE QUESTIONS ON THE NEXT PAGE!

Get ready for the second half!

6

Where can you stock up on itching powder and fake snot?

- [ ] **A)** Tee–Hee's Prank Emporium
- [ ] **B)** Har Har's Joke Shop
- [ ] **C)** Jo King's Hall of Laughs
- [ ] **D)** Itching Powder? Who needs it?

7

Who works in Beanotown's Top Secret Reseach Station?

- [ ] **A)** Professor Von Screwtop
- [ ] **B)** Dr Pfooflepfeffer
- [ ] **C)** Colonel Chemistry
- [ ] **D)** Lord Snooty

8

Where should you go if you're injured?

- [ ] **A)** St. Nowhere Hospital
- [ ] **B)** St. Somewhere Hospital
- [ ] **C)** St. Whichever Hospital
- [ ] **D)** St. Whodunnit Hospital

9

It's a bird! It's a plane! No, wait –
it's Beanotown's superhero . . .

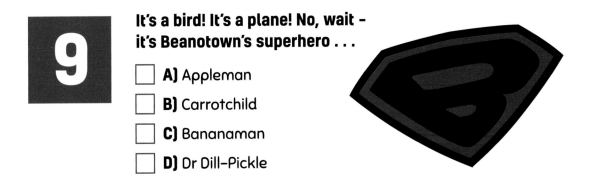

- [ ] **A)** Appleman
- [ ] **B)** Carrotchild
- [ ] **C)** Bananaman
- [ ] **D)** Dr Dill-Pickle

10

How many school rules are there for
you to break at Bash Street School?

- [ ] **A)** 1
- [ ] **B)** 10
- [ ] **C)** 100
- [ ] **D)** 923

AND A BONUS QUESTION:

11

What should you pack for your trip to Beanotown?

- [ ] **A)** This book. Pleeeease say this book. Otherwise,
  why did we waste 85 years writing it?

- [ ] **B)** An anti-pranking detector, because someone
  will probably try to prank you.

- [ ] **C)** A whoopee cushion, because you will probably
  want to try to prank someone else.

- [ ] **D)** All of the above!

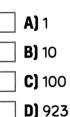

THAT'S ALL FOLKS! TO FIND OUT IF YOU'RE A
BEANO EXPERT TURN THE PAGE!

THE BIG BEANOTOWN QUIZ!

Answers

HOW DID YOU GET ON?

1 **B)** Vikings

2 **C)** Beanotown Museum

3 **D)** Wilbur Brown

4 **A)** That was totally **BLAM!!**

5 **C)** No.51... GASWORKS ROAD

6 **B)** Har Har's Joke Shop

7 **A)** Professor Von Screwtop

8 **B)** St. Somewhere Hospital

9 **C)** Bananaman

10 **D)** 923

Bonus Question

11 **D)** All of the above, of course!

Check out your score on the Bean-o-meter!

BEAN-O-METER

11	BEANOTOWN BOSS
10 **9** **8**	BEANOTOWN BOFFIN
7 **6** **5** **4**	BEANOTOWN BANG AVERAGE
3 **2** **1**	BEANOTOWN BLUFFER
0	BEANOTOWN BOZO

BECOME A BEANOTOWN RESIDENT

Now you've learned all there is to know about Beanotown and the people who live there, it's time to decide what sort of resident would you be! Fill in this character profile and come and join the Beanotown fun (unless this isn't your book – let's not anger any friends or librarians, shall we?)!

NAME: ....

Age: ....

Beanotown Address: ....

....

Draw a picture of your Beanotown alter-ego here

Known associates: ....
....
....

Motto: ....

....

Likes: ....

....

Dislikes: ....

....

Signature prank: ....

....

....

Super skills: ....

....

Parent/Guardian's signature: Just Kidding!
You don't need permission to be a
citizen of Beanotown!

MISCHIEF-O-METER

MEGA STINK BOMB

GOODBYE!

A trip to Beanotown is the gateway to loads of exciting, unpredictable opportunities. The one thing that you can say for sure is that you can't actually be sure what's going to happen.

We can't wait to see you back here in Beanotown again one day, now that you've discovered just how blamazing it really is!

Reviews for this awesome guide:

'Dear Ms Daley, thank you for your guide to Beanotown. Now I know all the places to avoid. Phew!'

Les D'Gruntled

'Another travel guide? What's the point? Why not just sit still – I can be pranked in my own house for free.'

Dusty Foyay

'You told me that if I came to Beanotown, I'd slip on a fake poo, be chased by an evil carrot and then fall down a trapdoor in the school basement. I'll have you know it was an evil cucumber that chased me – you should check your facts better next time!'

Petra Petty-Pants

PREVIOUSLY IN BEANOTOWN...

BEANO
WHERE'S GNASHER?

Gnee-hee! You'll gnever find me!

A BARKING MAD SEARCH AND FIND

BEANO
JOKE BOOK

BEANOTOWN'S BEST JOKES!

BEANO
WOULD YOU RATHER?

WITH OVER 200 BRAIN-BENDING CHOICES!

100% FUNNY! GUARANTEED!

FOR EVEN MORE FUN, HEAD TO BEANO.COM

DON'T MISS OUT ON THESE HILARIOUSLY FUN BOOKS!